Better Homes and Gardens®

Wiring

D0117181

Meredith® Books
Des Moines, Iowa

Table of contents

Introduction

Troubleshooting and Repair

Tools and Materials

Wiring Techniques

UPGRADES AND PROJECTS

Better Homes and Gardens® Wiring
Editor: Larry Johnston
Copy Chief: Terri Fredrickson
Copy Editor: Kevin Cox
Publishing Operations Manager: Karen Schirm
Senior Editor, Asset & Information Management: Phillip Morgan
Edit and Design Production Coordinator: Mary Lee Gavin
Editorial and Design Assistant: Renee E. McAtee
Book Production Managers: Pam Kvitne, Marjorie J. Schenkelberg,
   Rick von Holdt, Mark Weaver
Imaging Center Operator: Chris Sprague
Contributing Copy Editor: Don Gulbrandsen
Contributing Proofreaders: Cheri Madison, Michael Maine,
   Kristin McCullough
Contributing Indexer: Don Glassman
Other Contributors: Janet Anderson

Additional Editorial Contributions from
Abramowitz Creative Studios
Publishing Director/Designer: Tim Abramowitz
Designer/Illustrator: Kelly Bailey
Designer: Joel Wires
Photography: Image Studios
   Account Executive: Lisa Egan
   Photographer: Bill Rein
   Assistants: Mike Clines, Mike Croatt, Max Hermans,
      Bill Kapinski, Roger Wilmers
   Technical Advisor: Rick Nadke

Meredith® Books
Editor in Chief: Gregory H. Kayko
Executive Director, Design: Matt Strelecki
Managing Editor: Amy Tincher-Durik
Executive Editor/Group Manager: Benjamin W. Allen
Senior Associate Design Director: Tom Wegner
Marketing Product Manager: Brent Wiersma

Executive Director, Marketing: Kevin Kacere
Editorial Director: Linda Raglan Cunningham
Executive Director, New Business Development: Todd M. Davis
Director, Marketing & Publicity: Amy Nichols
Executive Director, Sales: Ken Zagor
Director, Operations: George A. Susral
Director, Production: Douglas M. Johnston
Business Director: Jim Leonard

Vice President and General Manager: Douglas J. Guendel

Meredith Publishing Group
President: Jack Griffin
Senior Vice President: Karla Jeffries

Meredith Corporation
Chairman of the Board: William T. Kerr
President and Chief Executive Officer: Stephen M. Lacy

In Memoriam: E. T. Meredith III (1933–2003)

All of us at Meredith® Books are dedicated to providing you with the information and ideas you need to enhance your home and garden. We welcome your comments and suggestions. Write to us at:
Meredith Books
Home Improvement Books Department
1716 Locust St.
Des Moines, IA 50309–3023

Note to the Readers: Due to differing conditions, tools, and individual skills, Meredith Corporation assumes no responsibility for any damages, injuries suffered, or losses incurred as a result of following the information published in this book. Before beginning any project, review the instructions carefully, and if any doubts or questions remain, consult local experts or authorities. Because codes and regulations vary greatly, you always should check with authorities to ensure that your project complies with all applicable local codes and regulations. Always read and observe all of the safety precautions provided by manufacturers of any tools, equipment, or supplies, and follow all accepted safety procedures.

Home electrical systems

Electricity is the flow of electrons through a conductor. In home electrical systems wires made of highly conductive copper wrapped in insulation for safety are the conductors that carry electricity.

Electricity always flows in a loop, known as a circuit. When a circuit is interrupted at any point, electricity ceases to flow. As soon as the circuit is reconnected, the flow begins again.

Your local electric company distributes electricity generated at power plants. Overhead and underground wires bring power from the utility company lines to a home's service head. (This is also called a weather head because it keeps rain and snow from entering.) Although the utility company sends high-voltage electricity along some of its power lines, by the time it reaches your house, it has been reduced to 120 volts.

The electricity passes through an electric meter, which measures how much power is consumed, into a service panel (also called the breaker box or fuse box), which distributes electricity throughout the house along individual circuits. Each circuit flows out of the service panel, through a number of fixtures and receptacles, and back to the service panel. (For more on service panels, see pages 8–9.)

In a circuit electricity flows out of the service panel on hot conductors that usually have black insulation, although sometimes they may be red or other colors. Electricity returns to the panel through neutral conductors that have white insulation.

The service panel contains circuit breakers or fuses. These safety devices shut off the power in case of a short circuit or other fault in the circuit (see pages 8–9, 24–25).

Each circuit has branches, which might include receptacles, lighting fixtures, or switches. A wall switch, for example, interrupts (turns off) or completes (turns on) the flow of

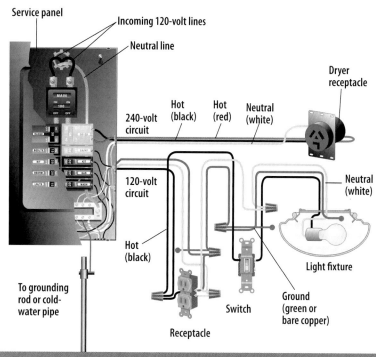

Service panel — **Incoming 120-volt lines** — **Neutral line** — **Dryer receptacle** — **240-volt circuit** — **Hot (black)** — **Hot (red)** — **Neutral (white)** — **120-volt circuit** — **Neutral (white)** — **Hot (black)** — **Light fixture** — **To grounding rod or cold-water pipe** — **Switch** — **Ground (green or bare copper)** — **Receptacle**

Following the flow

In a typical household system, a pair of 120-volt lines and a single neutral line enter the top of the service panel. A 240-volt circuit is fed by both 120-volt hot lines and the neutral lead. A 120-volt circuit is fed by a single 120-volt hot line and the neutral lead. Each circuit has a ground wire too, usually bare copper or green-insulated. In case of a short, the ground wire carries the current safely into the earth.

electricity to one or more light fixtures. Some appliances, such as a dishwasher, disposal, or microwave oven, have separate circuits.

Most home circuits carry 120 volts. This will give you quite a jolt if you accidentally come into contact with it, so you should always work around electrical systems with care. Most homes also have one or two 240-volt circuits, which use two hot wires and one neutral wire. Be especially cautious when dealing with these higher-power lines.

Every electrical system should be grounded for safety. Usually this is done by connecting a wire from the service panel to a cold-water pipe or a grounding rod sunk deep into the earth. Sometimes both grounds are used. Grounding diverts current harmlessly into the earth in case of a circuit fault.

Circuits in your home may have a grounding wire that is bare copper or green. Some fixtures and devices are grounded through the metal receptacle boxes and the metal conduit that contains the wires (see page 7).

Metal items, such as tools, and your body can also conduct electricity, often with harmful results. Keeping the electrical system in good order and working safely around it will help prevent this from happening.

Shutting off power

The primary rule of safe electrical work is simple but vital: Before touching or working with any wiring, always shut off the power, then test to make sure the power is off.

This page shows the most common ways to shut off power and test for power using a voltage tester. See pages 14–15 for other types of testers. You may want to use a voltage detector to double-check or to test for power before you open a box.

Take steps to remove all distractions while you work on wiring. Keep children away from the area where you are working. Focus on the task at hand.

To be doubly safe act as though the power is on even when you know it is off. Wear gym shoes or other shoes with rubber soles. Use tools made specifically for electrical work. These typically have generous rubber grips, so you never need to touch metal. Remove any jewelry, rings, or a watch. If you are working in the basement, stand on a wooden platform or rubber mat rather than the concrete floor, especially if it is wet. Use a nonconducting ladder (fiberglass is a good choice) rather than a metal ladder.

Shut off power to a single circuit

In most cases it is sufficient to shut off power only to the circuit being worked on. To do this flip a breaker or remove a fuse. (See pages 8–9 for more information about the service panel.) If your service panel is well labeled, you can easily find the circuit. Be aware, however, that the label may be incorrect, so always test for power after turning it off.

Shut off power to all circuits

For major projects, or if you are unsure which breaker or fuse controls the wiring you will work on, shut off power to the entire house. In most cases the main breaker or fuse is located at the top of the panel. Be aware that even after you have shut off the main breaker, the wires entering the box from outside the house are still live.

See that the power stays off

To ensure that nobody restores power while you work, tape a note to the box. For greater security lock the panel; most service panels have a place for a padlock.

Test for power

Test a receptacle for power by inserting a voltage tester's probes into the slots. You can also use a receptacle analyzer or a multitester. To test a switch's wiring, a ceiling fixture, or a junction box for power, remove the cover as shown on page 13 and touch the probes to the bare ends of the neutral wire and hot wire.

Grounding and polarization

Older homes often have ungrounded receptacles and fixtures, and many local codes do not require rewiring them so they're grounded. Grounding is still worth adding to your system, though, because it adds protection against electrical shock. Grounding provides a third path for electricity to travel along, so if there is a leak, current will flow into the earth rather than into the body of a person who touches a defective fixture, appliance, or tool.

An electrical system is grounded with a grounding rod driven at least 8 feet into the earth outside the house or connected to a cold-water pipe. Each individual branch circuit must be grounded as well, either with a separate wire that leads to the neutral bus bar of the service panel or through metal conduit or cable sheathing that runs without a break from each box to the panel.

In some locations in your house—especially where the outlet or appliances may become wet—GFCI (ground fault circuit interrupter) receptacles are required (see pages 86–87). Older, ungrounded circuits are usually polarized, which is less effective than grounding but better than nothing. Grounded and polarized receptacles provide protection only when wired correctly. Use a receptacle analyzer to test for this (page 37).

CAUTION

DON'T ALTER PRONGS ON PLUGS
Never clip or file down the prongs on a grounded or polarized plug. Go to the heart of the problem: Test and upgrade your circuit and receptacle.

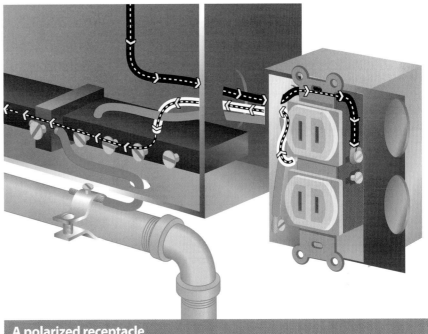

A polarized receptacle

A polarized outlet has one slot that is longer than the other. This ensures that when a polarized plug is inserted, the hot and neutral wires in the cord connect to the correct wires in the circuit. Although not as safe as a grounded system, polarization adds a measure of safety.

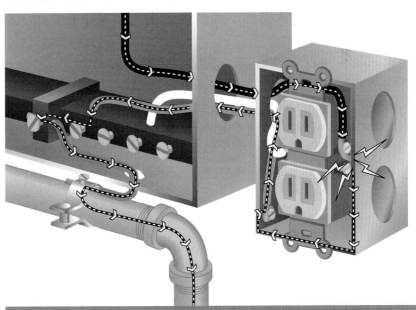

A grounded receptacle

The grounding circuit must follow an unbroken path to the earth. A third, rounded prong on modern plugs fits into the ground slot in the receptacle. This slot connects to a wire—or to the metal box and conduit or sheathing—that leads uninterrupted to the neutral bus bar of the breaker box. The system ground wire then connects the bus bar to the earth. Often a cold-water pipe is used for grounding instead of a grounding rod because it connects to water supply pipes deep under the ground.

Service panels

Electrical projects always begin at the service panel, which is either a circuit-breaker box or a fuse box. When a short or an overload shuts down power to a circuit, this is where you go to restore the flow. It's also where you cut off power to a circuit before starting a project.

Power arrives from the meter through two main power wires, each carrying 120 volts into the house. Usually these are black and red. A white main neutral wire completes the circuit. These incoming hot wires connect to a main power shutoff. When you turn this off, the incoming wires above the main shutoff remain hot, but there is no power to the fuses or breakers for branch circuits.

Breaker boxes
A breaker box's main shutoff connects to two hot bus bars. Each 120-volt breaker attaches to one of the bars. (This means that if one of the main hot wires gets damaged outside your house, you will lose power to about half of the circuits in your house.) Each 240-volt breaker attaches to both bus bars. When a circuit is overloaded or a short occurs, an element in the breaker heats up and causes the breaker to trip and shut off power before the wires heat up and become a danger.

The main neutral wire connects to the neutral bus bar. This bar is connected to a system ground wire, which leads to a grounding rod. White wires for every circuit, and sometimes bare or green ground wires, connect to the neutral bus bar. As a result each 120-volt circuit has a black or colored wire leading from a circuit breaker and a white wire leading to the neutral bus bar. A bare copper or green-covered ground wire may also connect to the neutral bus bar. Each 240-volt circuit has two hot wires connected to the circuit breaker. The 240-volt circuit also has one neutral and, possibly, a ground wire, connected to the neutral bus bar. Systems with conduit or armored cable do not necessarily need separate ground wires—the conduit or metal sheathing can act as the ground conductor.

Instructions for troubleshooting circuit breakers and checking for the cause of shorts are on page 24.

CAUTION

LEAVE INCOMING WIRES FOR THE UTILITY COMPANY

If you suspect that the wires entering your house may be damaged, do not attempt to work on them yourself. Have the utility company inspect them. Usually they will inspect and repair them for free.

Fuse boxes

If you have an older home that has not been rewired in the last 25 years, its electrical heart is probably a fuse box.

Fuse boxes are wired and work the same way as breaker boxes (opposite page), but instead of tripping as a breaker does, a fuse "blows" when there's too much current in its circuit. When this happens you must eliminate the short or the overload, remove the blown fuse, and screw in or plug in a new one.

As with a breaker box, electricity enters through two main power wires. (In a house with no 240-volt equipment, there may be only one power line.) The current flows through a main disconnect, in this case a pullout block that holds a pair of cartridge fuses.

A series of plug fuses protects the hot wires of the individual circuits, often called branch circuits. Unscrewing a fuse disconnects its circuit. A neutral bus bar receives the main neutral wire as well as all the neutral wires for the branch circuits. A system ground wire leads from the neutral bus bar to a grounding rod outside the house.

For tips on troubleshooting a fuse box, see page 25.

Main neutral wire

Main power wires

Neutral bus bar

Plug fuses

System ground wire

Pullout block

Cartridge fuse

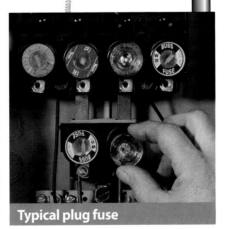

Typical plug fuse

A plug fuse is threaded and screws into the fuse box. Handle only the rim. Do not touch the threads while removing or replacing the fuse. For information on identifying and replacing a blown fuse, see page 25.

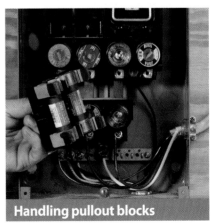

Handling pullout blocks

Larger 240-volt circuits, as well as main shutoff fuses, often are protected by pullout blocks that contain cartridge fuses. If you need to pull out a cartridge fuse that is not in a pullout block, do not use your fingers—you could touch the live end. Get a fuse puller (see page 25).

Household circuits

The electrical service in your house is divided into branch circuits. Each branch circuit supplies power to a particular area of your home. You must make sure that no branch circuit carries too great a load, or you will be constantly resetting breakers or replacing fuses. Some appliances need a dedicated separate circuit. An electric stove or clothes dryer, for instance, will have its own 240-volt circuit; other appliances may require their own 120-volt circuits. More often a circuit supplies a number of outlets. Some circuits serve both lights and outlets.

To find out if a circuit is overloaded, add up the total power drawn by the circuit, as outlined below. Check the breaker or fuse to see how many amps the circuit can deliver. If your total use exceeds the amperage the circuit can supply, change your usage. The solution may be as simple as plugging one of your appliances into a different receptacle. Or you may have to add another circuit. For extra safety limit the total load on a circuit to 80 percent of the breaker value—a 16-amp load on a 20-amp breaker, for instance.

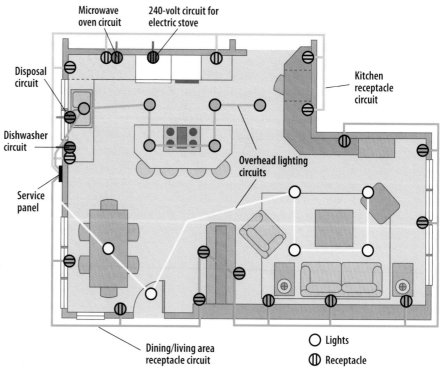

Microwave oven circuit

240-volt circuit for electric stove

Disposal circuit

Dishwasher circuit

Service panel

Kitchen receptacle circuit

Overhead lighting circuits

Dining/living area receptacle circuit

○ Lights

◍ Receptacle

Typical circuit plan

A well-planned electrical system has branch circuits that serve easily defined areas or purposes. Unfortunately many homes—especially those that have been remodeled several times—have circuits that roam all over the house. Note that some appliances, such as the microwave oven, dishwasher, and disposal, have their own circuits. The electric stove has a separate 240-volt circuit. Other circuits are roughly organized by the rooms they serve and their anticipated demand.

CIRCUIT LOADS

To figure your circuit loads, add up the watts being used. Check the specification label on each appliance. Also note the wattage of the lightbulbs in fixtures on the circuit. Some labels indicate watts as volt-amps (VA). Watts equals volts times amps, so divide the total wattage by 120 (the circuit voltage) to find out how many amperes (amps) the circuit draws when all the appliances and lights are on. This will help you determine whether you are placing too great a demand on a circuit. At right are some typical wattage and amperage figures for common household appliances.

Refrigerator:
500 watts/4.2 amps
Microwave oven:
800 watts/6.7 amps
7,500-Btu air-conditioner:
1,000 watts/8.1 amps
Toaster:
1,050 watts/8.75 amps
Gas dryer:
720 watts/6 amps
Washer:
600 watts/5 amps
Circular saw:
1,200 watts/10 amps

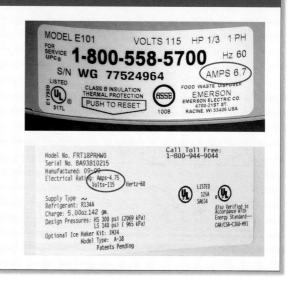

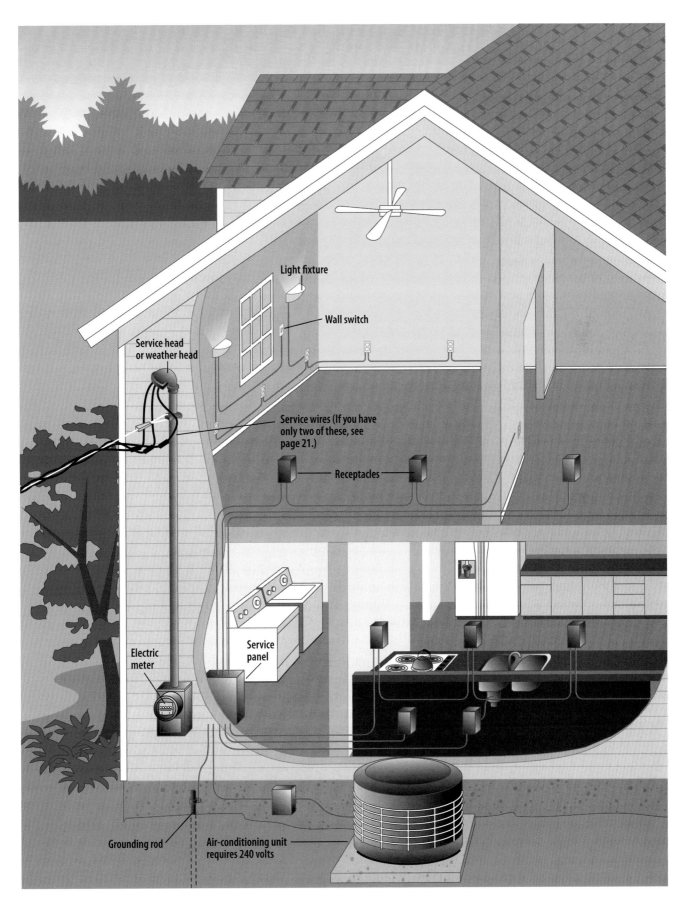

Light fixture

Wall switch

Service head
or weather head

Service wires (If you have
only two of these, see
page 21.)

Receptacles

Electric
meter

Service
panel

Grounding rod

Air-conditioning unit
requires 240 volts

Mapping your circuits

Is there a chart inside the door of your service panel showing which circuits each breaker controls? If not, make one. You'll be glad you mapped the circuits the next time you have to turn off a circuit for repairs or improvements or when you have to find a tripped breaker.

Begin by making a sketch of each floor in the house, showing all receptacles, switches, appliances, and fixtures. Remember that 240-volt receptacles will have their own circuits. You may have to make more than one drawing per floor for a large house.

Have a helper flip switches and test outlets while you stay at the box and write down the findings. If you work alone plug in a radio turned to peak volume to find the general area covered by the circuit. The radio will go silent when you switch off the circuit. Then test other outlets to find all of them on that circuit.

1 Test each outlet

Number the circuit breakers or fuses. Turn on all the appliances and lights on one floor. Plug a lamp into every receptacle. Turn off one circuit and have your helper write the breaker number on the map next to each outlet that went dead.

2 Make a record on the service panel

Test every circuit for each floor. Write the findings on a sheet of paper and tape it to the inside of the service panel door.

CAUTION

HANDLE YOUR SERVICE PANEL WITH RESPECT

Take special care when working around a service panel. Remove cover plates only when you absolutely have to, and replace them as soon as you can. Keep the door shut whenever you are not inspecting the panel—lock it if you think kids may get at it. Remember that even if you have shut off the main power breaker or switch, there is still power entering the box.

3 Make a load sheet

To really understand how your house uses electricity, combine the information from circuit mapping with power-use information from appliance labels. Write up a load sheet as shown. It will help you assess capacity for future additions to your electrical system.

THE NEC

Electrical codes are based on the National Electrical Code (NEC), which is published by a nonprofit organization and is upgraded periodically. The NEC covers every electrical situation and prescribes practices to ensure safety and reliability. It provides the model on which virtually all local building codes are based.

Some communities simply adopt the NEC as their own; others modify it. Any time you want to make a change in your electrical system, check the NEC and local codes before you begin.

Opening electrical boxes

I n a safe, code-approved electrical system, every wire connection is enclosed in an electrical box. Most electrical projects require that you open a box to get at the wiring. As long as you take the proper precautions, you can do this safely.

Shut off the electricity to the circuit and do a preliminary test for power: Use a tester to check a receptacle for power, or flip a switch to see if a light comes on. Be aware, however, that power may still be present in the box from another circuit even if the one you are working on is turned off. So proceed cautiously.

1 Remove the cover plate

After testing to see that the power is off, remove the cover plate's screws—one for a receptacle cover and two for a switch cover. If the cover plate does not come off easily, gently pry with the screwdriver, taking care not to poke the blade in more than ⅛ inch.

2 Pull out the device

Unscrew the mounting screws until the device is free (the screws will probably not come all the way out). Hold the device by the plastic part only and gently pull outward. Test all exposed wires for power; it is possible that power from another circuit is traveling through the box.

Open a junction box

Junction boxes often contain power from more than one circuit, so use a voltage detector to check all wires as well as the box itself (see page 14). The cover plate may be metal or plastic. You can remove one screw and loosen the other to remove the cover plate. Once it is open, double-check for power using a voltage tester.

Open a ceiling fixture

After flipping the switch to see that the power is off (make sure it's not just a burned-out bulb), loosen the setscrews and remove the glass or plastic globe. Remove the bulbs. Usually the canopy is held in place by either two mounting screws or a center nut. Remove the screws or nut and gently pull the fixture down. If it is heavy support it with a coat hanger (see page 90).

Open a service panel

Open the panel's door and flip off the main breaker or remove the main fuse. To get at the panel's wires, remove the mounting screws, which may be on the face of the cover or on the sides of the box. Remove the cover.

Using testers

Keep a reliable voltage tester close at hand at all times and make it a habit to test for power at the beginning of every project.

Become comfortable using your tester so you can make firm contact with both probes while looking at the tester's indicator. In many cases you'll have to hold both the tester and one probe, or both probes with one hand. Alternatively you can allow the tester to dangle while you hold one probe in each hand.

Be sure both probes make firm contact with bare wire or other metal—not the plastic insulation. If the metal is painted, test, then scrape the paint away, then test again. When testing a receptacle insert the probes all the way in.

Receptacle analyzer

Just plug it in. A receptacle analyzer will tell you if the power is on and whether the receptacle is properly grounded and polarized (see page 7).

Voltage tester

For standard 120-volt power, touch the probes of a voltage tester to one black (or colored) wire and the white wire (or the terminals the wires are connected to); or to the black wire and the electrical box, if it is metal.

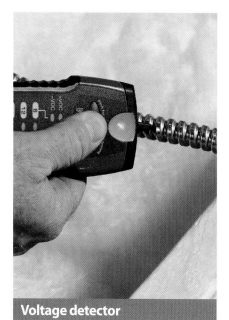

Voltage detector

Hold a voltage detector near or up against an electrical box, a fixture, or a cable. When you press the button, the detector will glow if power is present. A voltage detector can often sense power inside a wall, but not always.

Electronic scanner

A multifunction scanner senses the presence of studs, pipes, and electrical cables inside a wall. It can also act like a voltage detector, telling you if power is present in cables. If you have plaster walls (rather than drywall), it may not give reliable readings.

Testing a 240-volt receptacle

Use a four-level tester or a multitester to check a 240-volt receptacle. When you insert the probes into the receptacle's two vertical slots, the tester should register 240 volts. Inserting into one vertical slot and one other slot should yield a reading of 120 volts.

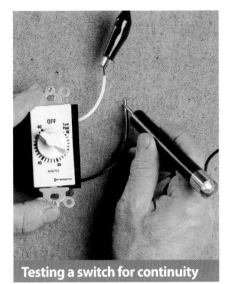

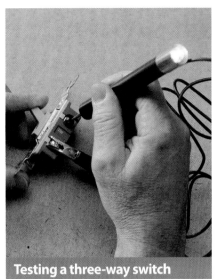

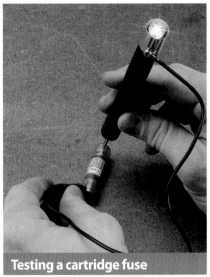

Testing a switch for continuity

Disconnect power before using a continuity tester. To test a two-way switch or a special switch (see pages 50–51), clip one tester lead to one terminal or wire end and touch the probe to the other terminal or wire end. The tester should glow when the switch is turned on and not glow when the switch is off; otherwise replace the switch.

Testing a three-way switch

To test a three-way switch, fasten the tester's clip to the dark common screw terminal and touch the probe to one of the other terminals. If the tester glows when you flip the switch to one position and stops glowing when you flip it to the other position, the switch works properly. Test both terminals.

Testing a cartridge fuse

Hold a continuity tester's clip against one end of a cartridge fuse and touch the probe to the other end. If the tester glows the fuse is good. If not, replace it.

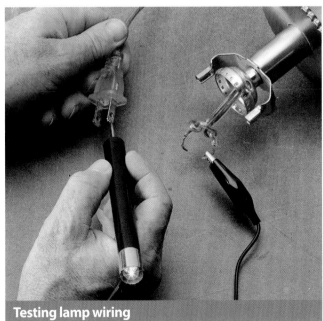

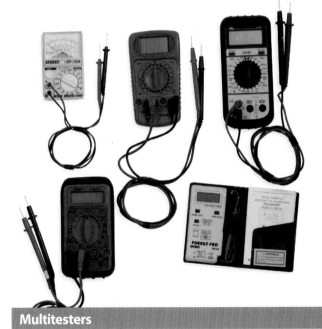

Testing lamp wiring

Dismantle a lamp and pull out the wires so you can tell where they travel. Using a continuity tester, clip one end of a wire and touch the other end with the probe. If the tester does not glow, the wire is broken somewhere and should be replaced.

Multitesters

A multitester performs several functions and can take the place of several testing devices. Use it to test 120-volt circuits, 240-volt circuits, and low-voltage wiring. It is an essential tool for some appliance repairs (not covered in this book) because it tells you precisely how much power is present. It also tests for continuity and resistance. A digital multitester is easier to read than an analog multitester.

Switch and receptacle wiring

The wiring you will see when you open a switch or receptacle box is not always straightforward at first glance. You will usually find several wires attached to a switch or receptacle. Wires enter the box and often exit the box to travel to a fixture or the next receptacle. This page and the next show some common ways switches and receptacles are wired.

GROUNDING METHODS

The wiring arrangements shown on these pages emphasize the hot and neutral wires. Also pay attention to how the devices are grounded. Receptacles should always be grounded. Grounding is recommended for switches and lights, but many systems omit this. If the device's box is plastic, a ground wire should connect to the device. If the box is metal, the most secure arrangement is to attach ground wires to both the device and the box. In some systems a ground wire attaches only to the device. If the circuit has metallic armored cable or metal conduit, the metal box can act as the ground, eliminating the need for a ground wire.

If your appliance or tool has a plug with a third, round prong, it should only be plugged into a properly grounded three-hole outlet (see opposite page). Some appliances and tools are double insulated and do not need the extra protection of a grounding prong. You can plug them into an ungrounded outlet and still be protected from an electrical shock.

Through-wired switch

If power comes into the switch box first and then goes to the fixture, the neutral (white) wire travels directly to the fixture, and the hot (black or colored) wire flows through the switch. When flipped on the switch allows power to flow; when flipped off it interrupts the flow of power.

End-wired switch

If power flows directly to the fixture, a two-wire cable leads from the fixture to the switch. One wire connects to the hot wire in the box, the other goes to the fixture's hot wire so power travels through the switch. The end of the white wire is colored black with an indelible marker to show it is hot in this wiring arrangement.

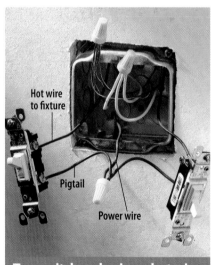

Hot wire to fixture

Pigtail

Power wire

Two switches sharing a hot wire

Usually two switches in the same room connect to the same circuit so they can share a single hot wire. All the neutral wires are spliced together. Power enters each switch via a pigtail—a short lead—from the black power wire.

Three-way switch wiring

Two three-way switches control the same fixture from two different locations. A three-way switch has three terminals (plus the terminal for the ground) and its toggle doesn't have On and Off markings. The hot wire connects to the common terminal, which is usually darker in color than the other terminals. For three-way wiring see pages 104–106.

Midrun receptacle

If two cables enter a receptacle box, one brings power to the receptacle and the other leads out to receptacles down the line. This is a midrun receptacle. The two neutral wires connect to the neutral (silver) terminals, and the two black wires connect to the hot (brass) terminals.

End-of-run receptacle

If only one cable enters a receptacle box, the receptacle is at the end of the run. Connect the white wire to the neutral (silver) terminal and the black wire to the hot (brass) terminal.

Split receptacle

When two hot wires run to the hot (brass) terminals, and the connecting tab between the two has been broken off, the receptacle is split. Either the receptacle's two outlets are each on a separate circuit so you can plug in two high-amperage appliances without overloading either circuit; or the receptacle is split and switched, meaning one of the outlets is controlled by a wall switch somewhere in the room.

Wire colors

A different color hot wire designates each circuit in homes that use wires in conduit rather than cable (see pages 78–81). This can help identify the circuit. If, for instance, a device is connected to a blue wire, look for a blue wire in the service panel to find the corresponding circuit breaker. Verify that the breaker does shut off the device before doing any work.

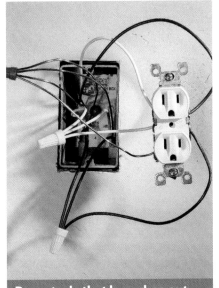

Receptacle that branches out

If three cables enter a box and all the wires connect to the receptacle, then it is a midrun receptacle that provides power for another branch or fixture. In other words power leaves the receptacle in two directions. The extra wires should be connected via pigtails; it is not safe to attach two wires to a single terminal.

WIRING ARRANGEMENTS YOU MIGHT FIND

Red and black wires. Sometimes a single three-wire cable—with a red, black, and white wire—is used to wire two different circuits. The red wire is the hot wire for one circuit, and the black is the hot wire for the other circuit. The white wire is used as a neutral for both circuits.

A receptacle with two hot wires. When two black wires or a black one and a red (or other color) one connect to the two brass (hot) terminals, the receptacle is split. Either each of its two outlets is connected to a different circuit, or one outlet is controlled by a wall switch and the other is always hot (see page 109).

Wires that travel through. If wires travel through a box but are not connected to the box's device or fixture, they probably are for a different circuit.

Inspecting your home's wiring

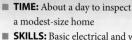

■ **TIME:** About a day to inspect a modest-size home
■ **SKILLS:** Basic electrical and wiring knowledge
■ **TOOLS:** Voltage tester, screwdriver

With a basic understanding of wiring, you can spot most of the problems that might be encountered in a home electrical system. The next three pages show some common problems you might find.

If you see a problem, shut off the power to the circuit, test to make sure the electricity is off, and correct the problem before restoring power. If you spot a wiring configuration that you do not understand, call a professional electrician for an evaluation. Do not change or work on any wiring you do not understand.

The point of attachment

Power enters your home either through a weather head, as shown, or an underground cable. Conduct a visual inspection but do not touch anything. Make sure the wires are firmly secured and the insulation is in good condition. Overhead wires should be high enough to avoid contact. If you see anything that might be a problem, call the electrical utility for an inspection.

Outdoor connections

From the point of entry, cables or conduit travel down your home's siding until they enter the house. The wiring travels through a meter, which may be inside or outside, and then goes to the service panel. All conduits and cables should be solidly attached to the house. The outdoor attachments should be watertight. If the wiring is within reach of children, make sure it is safe. Call the utility if you see any potential problems.

Missing knockout

Any exposed hole, such as this missing knockout in a basement switch box, is a serious danger. Children or even adults can easily poke a finger in and get a painful shock. Buy a knockout filler, also called a goof plug (see page 56), and anchor it firmly to fill the hole.

Cracked or missing cover plate

Protect all receptacles and switches with cover plates that are in good condition. If a cover plate is even slightly damaged, replace it.

Test a GFCI receptacle

GFCIs (see pages 86–87) can wear out. When that happens a GFCI will supply power but not protection. Test GFCIs every month. When you push the test button, the power should shut off. If not replace the device.

Damaged cord insulation

Cord insulation can become brittle and crack easily, especially if subjected to high heat. Cords are also easy to nick. A repair with electrician's tape is a temporary fix at best. To be safe replace the entire cord. Also replace any cracked or wobbly plugs (see pages 30–31).

Missing cable clamp

Cable clamps protect the cable connection from being pulled apart, help protect the insulation from nicks, and seal the box's hole. An unclamped cable is dangerous. See page 75 for ways to clamp cable.

Loose cable

Wherever cable is exposed (typically in a basement, garage, or attic), it should be tightly fastened with straps or staples specifically made for attaching wiring. Unsecured cables are susceptible to damage. And do not use cables as clotheslines or to otherwise support loads.

Overloaded receptacle

Plugging too many cords into a receptacle poses the risk of overloading a circuit. An arrangement like this also makes it easy to accidentally pull out a plug, and creates a tripping hazard. Install an additional receptacle and move some of the load to other circuits.

Bulb too big

It's tempting to install a 100-watt bulb in a fixture rated for only 60 watts, but doing so will cause the fixture to overheat dangerously. This may not start a fire, but the extra heat may partially melt insulation and cause it to become brittle. If you need more light, replace the fixture with one that has a higher wattage rating.

Bare bulb in a closet

A lightbulb, even a low-wattage one, gets hot, which is why modern codes require closet fixtures to have protective globes. If you don't have a globe, at least keep clothing and flammables a minimum of 1 foot away from the bulb. Better yet, install a new, safer fixture.

Receptacle wired incorrectly

Hot lead attached to neutral terminal

Whenever you open a box (see pages 13, 16–17), inspect the wiring. The wire ends should be attached firmly to terminal screws, and the insulation should be free of nicks. On a receptacle the white wire goes to the silver terminal, and the black wire connects to the brass terminal.

Crowded box

If a box contains so many wires that they have to be crammed in, overheating or shorts could result. Installing an extension ring might enlarge the box enough. Or replace the box with a larger one.

Loose ceiling fixture

A heavy ceiling fixture, such as a chandelier or a ceiling fan, should be attached to a fan-rated box, which is stronger than a normal ceiling box (see pages 112–113). If the fixture has come loose from the box, it is usually easy to reattach. If the box itself is loose, you may be able to secure it by driving screws into an abutting joist. Otherwise remove the fixture and install a new box.

ALUMINUM WIRING

During the early 1970s some homes were built using aluminum wiring. The tendency for aluminum wires to expand when hot and contract as they cool led to loose connections, so aluminum house wiring was discontinued. Aluminum wire is thicker than copper wire (14-gauge aluminum wire is the same diameter as 12-gauge copper wire) and usually has AL printed on the insulation. An aluminum-wired system can be safe, as long as its devices are rated for use with aluminum—they are labeled CO/ALR. If you splice a copper wire to an aluminum wire, be sure to apply antioxidant to the wires, then twist on a wire nut rated for use with aluminum wire. If an aluminum-to-aluminum splice comes loose, do the same.

Wrong breaker or fuse

In a service panel a 14-gauge wire should be connected to a 15-amp breaker or fuse, and a 12-gauge wire should be connected to a 20-amp breaker. If the amperage of a breaker or fuse is too high for the wire, the wiring could overheat dangerously before the breaker trips or the fuse blows. Replace the breaker or the fuse with one of the correct amperage.

Unsafe wire routing

In a service panel wires should run neatly around the perimeter inside the box. If wires are bunched together or close to electrical connections, shut off the main breaker or fuse and gently move them to the side. If you see charring or melted insulation, or if the wiring is badly disorganized, call an electrician to evaluate the conditions.

Problems with older systems

An older home may have an inadequate and unsafe electrical service. The wiring can be confusing as well. If you are unsure about your home's wiring, have a professional check it out.

Some older systems have only two wires—rather than three—entering the house from the utility company. This arrangement does not have the capacity to provide the 240-volt circuits needed for electric ranges, clothes dryers, and other appliances.

Modern residential electrical service provides at least 100 amps of power. This is enough to power a medium-size house with an average number of appliances. If your service panel provides less amperage and you often blow fuses, or if you want to add new circuits, see pages 136–137.

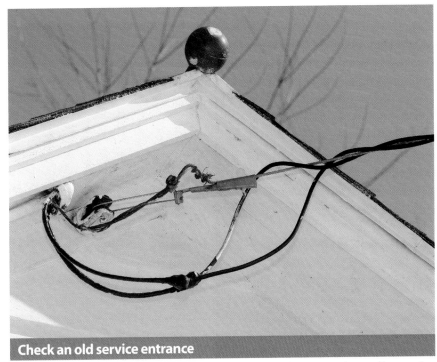

Check an old service entrance

A point of attachment like this lacks a modern watertight entrance head (see page 18). Chances are the utility company will install a better attachment if you call them. At least make sure the porcelain insulator is not cracked.

60-amp fuse box

A house built in the 1950s or before may have only 60-amp service and a fuse box that contains only four fuses. This small number of circuits limits how many fixtures and appliances you can safely run.

Damaged insulation

Old brittle wire insulation can easily crack, and the resulting exposed wire poses a danger. If the problem occurs only in a few spots, shut off the power and wrap the wire with electrician's tape. If much of the wiring is brittle, purchase special shrink-wrap sleeves made for protecting old wires.

DARKENED INSULATION

In some older homes cloth wire insulation has darkened to the point where you cannot tell a white (neutral) wire from a black (hot) wire. Sometimes this leads to incorrect wiring. If a switch is incorrectly wired into the neutral wire rather than the hot wire (see page 5), then the switch will turn off the light, but power will still be present in the hot wire in the fixture's box. To be safe flip the switch off and use a voltage detector to check for power in the fixture box.

Knob-and-tube wiring

Some or all of the wiring may be done with individual wires (rather than cable) routed through the framing with ceramic knobs and tubes. This wiring is generally safe if it is correctly installed and protected from damage or contact. But devices usually are not grounded (see page 7), so consider having an electrician rewire the home to update the system.

Older boxes

An old home with plaster ceilings may have pancake ceiling boxes like this. Wires often run through a center pipe, which may have been a gaslight line once. A box like this is usually not strong enough to hold a heavy chandelier or a ceiling fan. To attach a new fixture, you may need to buy special hardware (see pages 112–113).

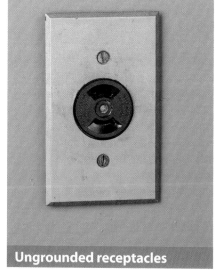

Ungrounded receptacles

If an old receptacle has only two slots and no ground hole, it is not grounded. If the receptacle can be grounded (see pages 7 and 36–37), replace it with a three-prong grounded receptacle. Otherwise install a two-prong ungrounded receptacle and do not plug in any appliance that has a three-prong plug.

IS THE REST OF THE WIRING SOUND?

In an older home the wiring in boxes may have dangerously brittle insulation, which may make you wonder about all the wiring you cannot see.

As long as the wires are encased in sheathing, you need not lie awake worrying about it. As long as the sheathing is in good shape, the encased wire insulation will last far longer than the insulation that is exposed to the air in boxes.

If your home has wires running through conduit, the wires will be somewhat exposed to the air. Fortunately it is possible to fish new wires through the conduit—a good idea for a system that is more than 60 years old.

Knob-and-tube wiring (above left) with insulation that is generally brittle should definitely be replaced; it is a serious fire hazard.

Nonpolarized receptacle

A receptacle with two slots the same length is not polarized, which is a hazardous situation (see page 7). Replace it with a polarized receptacle, connecting the neutral wire (white) to the silver terminal and the hot (black) wire to the brass one.

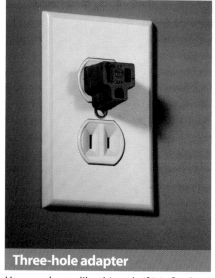

Three-hole adapter

Use an adapter like this only if it is firmly attached to the mounting screw and the mounting screw is grounded. Test the adapter with a receptacle analyzer to ensure that it is grounded. If it is not remove the adapter and use the receptacle only for two-prong plugs. If it is grounded replace the ungrounded receptacle with a grounded one.

TROUBLESHOOTING AND REPAIR

Circuit breakers

- **TIME:** A few seconds to reset a breaker; about 10 minutes per device to inspect for shorts
- **SKILLS:** No special skills needed
- **TOOLS:** Screwdriver

Think of a circuit breaker as a heat-sensing switch. As the illustrations, right, show, when the toggle is on, current flows through a set of contacts attached to a spring and lever. The contacts are held together by tension in the bimetal strip through which the current flows.

If there is a short or an overload in the circuit, the bimetal strip heats up and bends. As it bends it releases a lever that opens the spring-loaded contact. The contact remains open until the toggle is manually reset.

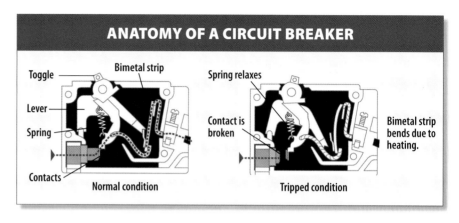

ANATOMY OF A CIRCUIT BREAKER

Toggle · Bimetal strip · Spring relaxes

Lever · Contact is broken · Bimetal strip bends due to heating.

Spring

Contacts

Normal condition · **Tripped condition**

Identifying tripped breakers and how to reset them

A tripped breaker is recognizable in any of the four ways shown at right. To find out whether the problem has corrected itself, reset the breaker. If the problem persists the breaker will shut itself off again. Usually the problem is an overload, and you only need to unplug or turn off one of the circuit's big energy users. If the circuit breaker keeps tripping even though it isn't overloaded, suspect a short. A defective plug, cord, or socket may be the problem.

Tripped position: center to reset, flip off, then on

Tripped position: off to reset, flip to on

Tripped position: red flag showing, switch in center to reset, flip off, then on

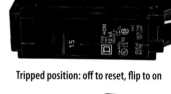

Tripped position: off to reset, press in and release

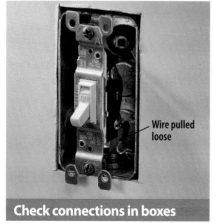

Check connections in boxes

Short circuits can occur in electrical boxes. Look for a loose wire that has shorted out against the box.

Wire pulled loose

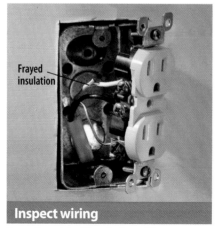

Inspect wiring

Frayed or nicked insulation will expose wire and could cause a short. Wrap damaged insulation with layers of electrical tape.

Frayed insulation

Watch for overheated fixtures

Heat can damage wire insulation and sockets. Never use bulbs with higher wattage ratings than recommended for the fixture.

Fuses

- **TIME:** 10 minutes to inspect your fuses
- **SKILLS:** Using continuity tester
- **TOOLS:** Fuse puller, continuity tester

Fuses serve the same purpose as circuit breakers. Instead of switching off the current as a breaker does, though, a fuse contains a strip of metal that melts when too much current flows in the circuit. When this happens you must eliminate the short or overload (see opposite page) and replace the blown fuse.

Solder-filled base takes a few seconds to melt and shut down the circuit.

Time-delay fuse

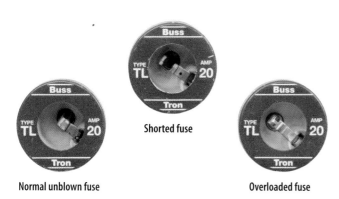

Shorted fuse

Normal unblown fuse

Overloaded fuse

Tamperproof fuse

Adapter

Spring-loaded tab prevents adapter from being unscrewed.

Understanding blown fuses

By examining a fuse you usually can tell what made it blow—an overload or a short. A short circuit usually explodes the strip, blackening the fuse window. An overload usually melts it, leaving the window clear.

Fuse options

A tamperproof fuse is an important safety device that makes it impossible to install a fuse with a higher amperage rating than the circuit is designed for. Its threaded adapter fits permanently into the fuse socket and accepts only a fuse with the proper rating.

When an electric motor on a washing machine or refrigerator starts up, it causes a momentary overload, which can blow fuses unnecessarily. A time-delay fuse avoids this problem—only a sustained overload will blow the fuse, not a brief surge.

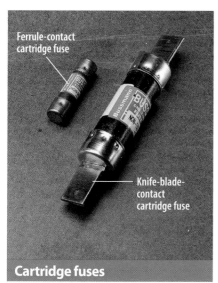

Ferrule-contact cartridge fuse

Knife-blade-contact cartridge fuse

Cartridge fuses

Ferrule-contact cartridge fuses handle 30- to 60-amp circuits. Knife-blade-contact fuses carry 70 amps or more. Handle both with extreme caution. Touching either in a live circuit with your bare hand could shock you.

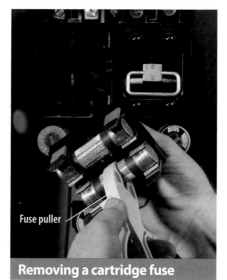

Fuse puller

Removing a cartridge fuse

For safety keep a plastic fuse puller with your spare fuses and use it as shown. Note, too, that the ends of a cartridge fuse get hot, so don't touch them immediately after you've pulled the fuse.

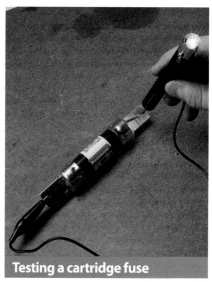

Testing a cartridge fuse

To see if a cartridge fuse has blown, check it with a continuity tester. Clamp or hold the clip on one end and touch the probe to the other. The bulb will light if the fuse is good.

Lightbulbs

When a lamp or light fixture quits working, the first thing to check is the lightbulb. Choosing the right replacement bulb is important.

A label on the lamp or light fixture shows the wattage limit for bulbs. A standard bulb of a higher wattage than recommended will overheat the fixture. This probably will not start an immediate fire, but it will likely damage the wire insulation or light sockets, possibly causing problems later. If you need more illumination, the best solution is to install a new fixture.

GO FOR LONGER LIFE

Standard incandescent bulbs cost the least, but bulbs labeled "long life" will usually more than pay for themselves. However incandescents are not very energy efficient. Fluorescents that screw into regular sockets last longer and use less energy. Most take a few seconds to become bright. If that is a problem, consider a halogen bulb, which is nearly as energy efficient but lights up immediately. Ensure that the fixture can take the heat generated by a halogen bulb.

Most household fixtures and lamps take a lightbulb with a medium base. Decorative fixtures or lamps may require bulbs with different-size bases.

For track and recessed lighting, choose a flood bulb for wide illumination or a spot bulb to highlight a small area.

Halogen fixtures use low voltage, and only low-voltage halogen bulbs will work in them. Flood and spot bulbs are available for halogens. Be aware that halogen bulbs get very hot.

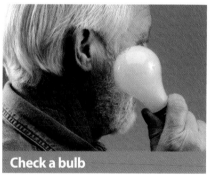

Check a bulb

If a light fixture or lamp suddenly stops lighting, you probably just need to change the bulb. First try screwing it in; it may be loose. If a bulb flickers even when screwed in tight, the light fixture may have a loose wire connection. Unscrew the bulb, hold it next to your ear, and jiggle it. A burned-out bulb usually tinkles audibly.

Removing a broken bulb

If a bulb is broken, **shut off the power to the circuit.** Depending on how much of the glass envelope remains, you may be able to grip the bulb by inserting a broom handle or other piece of wood into the center of the bulb.

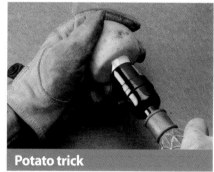

Potato trick

If a broomstick does not do the job, try jabbing the broken shards with a potato. After unscrewing throw away the potato and the bulb base.

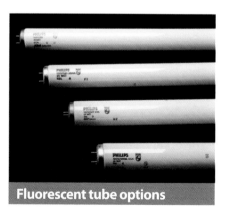

Fluorescent tube options

Fluorescent lighting doesn't need to feel cold and industrial. Home centers carry a variety of fluorescent lighting choices, ranging from the coldest (and cheapest) to the very warm. Tubes labeled "full spectrum" or "daylight" deliver illumination similar to sunlight. Grow-light tubes mimic sunlight even more closely and can help indoor plants thrive.

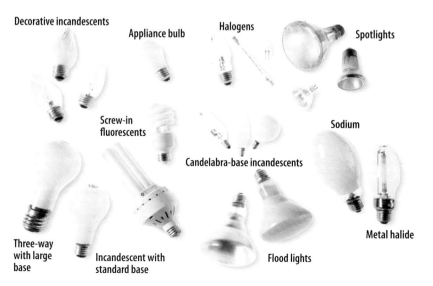

Decorative incandescents

Appliance bulb

Halogens

Spotlights

Screw-in fluorescents

Sodium

Candelabra-base incandescents

Three-way with large base

Incandescent with standard base

Flood lights

Metal halide

Incandescent fixtures

- **TIME:** About ½ hour to inspect a typical fixture
- **SKILLS:** No special skills needed
- **TOOLS:** Screwdriver, continuity tester

Though they vary in style, most incandescent fixtures have the same components.

Mounting screws hold a canopy plate against the ceiling. The canopy has one or more sockets for bulbs. A translucent diffuser or globe reduces the glare of bare bulbs. In newer fixtures fiber insulation provides added protection from heat damage to the wires and ceiling. Although it makes installation a bit more difficult, don't remove the fiber insulation.

If a fixture shorts out, causing a circuit to blow and/or creating sparks, the problem is probably in the fixture. If it simply refuses to light, the wall switch may be faulty (see pages 34–35).

CAUTION

USE THE RIGHT BULBS

A label on the fixture lists the maximum bulb wattage allowed. Don't install higher-wattage bulbs. Your fixture will overheat, burn out bulbs quickly, and become dangerous.

1 Inspect the socket

Shut off the circuit that powers the fixture. Inspect the socket. If it is cracked, or if the wires are scorched or melted, replace the socket or the entire fixture. Remove the bulb and check the contact at the socket's base. If it's corroded scrape the contact with a flat screwdriver or steel wool and pry it up.

2 Check the wiring

If the problem remains loosen the mounting screws and drop the fixture from its box. Check for loose connections and damaged wires. Slightly peeling drywall paper or heat-cracked wire insulation means an overheated fixture. Reduce the wattage of the bulbs or replace the fixture. Wrap any bare wires with electrical tape.

Troubleshooting a chandelier

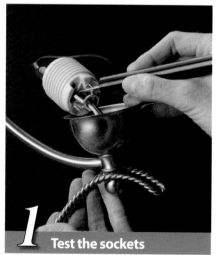

1 Test the sockets

Shut off power to the circuit. Test the sockets of nonworking lights. Attach the continuity tester to the socket's metal threads and touch the probe to the white-wire terminal. The tester should light. Test between the contact in the bottom of the socket and the black-wire terminal.

2 Test the wires

Remove the chandelier. Determine where all the cords run; you may need to open a junction box where all the wires converge. To test the wires that run to each socket, check each black wire from the junction box to the hot contact inside the socket and each white wire to the socket shell.

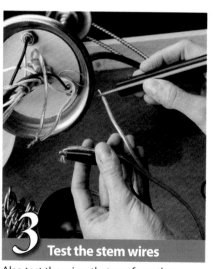

3 Test the stem wires

Also test the wires that run from the fixture's canopy to the junction box. If you need to replace the wire, tape the new wire to the old one. Then pull out the old wire until the new wire comes through.

Fluorescent fixtures

■ **TIME:** About 1 hour to inspect a fixture
and replace a ballast (for example)
■ **SKILLS:** No special skills needed
■ **TOOLS:** Screwdriver

The heart of an older fluorescent fixture is its ballast, a transformer that steps up voltage and sends it to a pair of lamp holders. The current passes through the lamp holders and excites a gas inside the fluorescent tube, causing its phosphorus-coated inner surface to glow with cool, diffused light.

Compared to incandescent bulbs, fluorescent tubes produce less heat, last longer, and consume less electricity. However problems with the fixtures sometimes arise. The ballast in a fixture can burn out after years of steady use, and the lamp holders can crack easily if they get bumped. Starters in very old units must be replaced periodically.

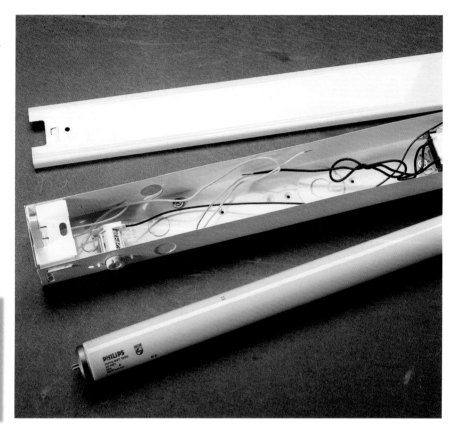

CAUTION

SAFE DISPOSAL
Never get rid of burned out tubes by breaking them. They contain mercury. Dispose of them whole or ask local authorities for disposal guidelines.

1 Wiggle the tube

Fluorescent tubes rarely burn out abruptly. If a tube suddenly stops lighting, try wiggling and rotating the ends of the tube to make sure it's properly seated.

2 Change a worn-out tube

A working tube usually has a grayish tinge near its ends. If the ends turn dark gray or black, the tube is failing and should be replaced. Purchase a tube that is the same length and wattage as the old one. If the tube is uniformly dim, it may simply need washing. To wash a tube remove it from the fixture, wipe it with a damp cloth, and then replace the tube.

3 Replace the starter

Older, delayed-start fluorescent lights flicker momentarily as they light up. If the flickering continues for more than a few seconds, make sure the starter is seated properly. Push it in and turn it clockwise. When the ends of a tube light up but its center does not, the starter is defective. Press the starter in and turn it counterclockwise to remove it.

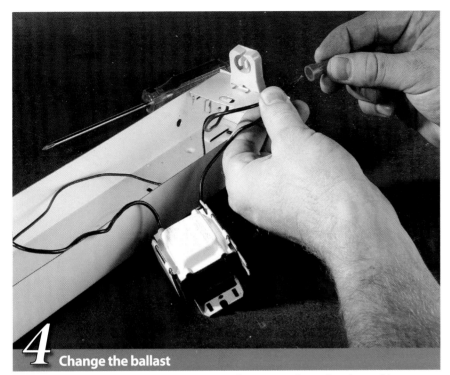

4 Change the ballast

If the fixture hums or oozes a tarlike goop, the ballast needs replacing. (Compare prices; you may be better off replacing the entire unit.) To remove the ballast shut off the power to the fixture, then release the wires at the sockets by pushing a screwdriver into the release openings. Unscrew the ballast and disconnect the wires to the power source. Reassemble with the new ballast.

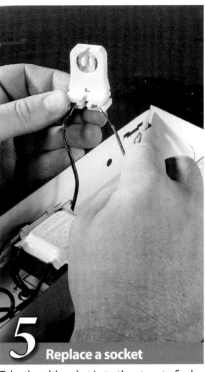

5 Replace a socket

Take the old socket in to the store to find a replacement that will fit. Strip ¾ inch of insulation from each wire end and poke the wires into the socket's terminal holes.

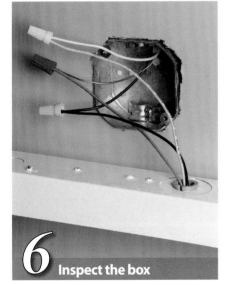

6 Inspect the box

If these steps don't solve the problem, you may not have power going into the fixture. Remove the fixture and look for loose connections and broken or bare wires in the outlet box.

TROUBLESHOOTING FLUORESCENT FIXTURES

Symptom	Solution
Tube does not light	1. Rotate the tube to make sure it is properly seated.
	2. Replace any damaged lamp holders.
	3. Replace the starter, if there is one.
	4. Check the wall switch and outlet box to see that there is power to the fixture.
Tube flickers or only lights partially	1. Rotate the tube to make sure it is properly seated.
	2. Replace any tubes that are discolored or have damaged pins.
	3. Replace the starter, if there is one.
Black substance or humming sound	1. Replace the ballast or the entire fixture.

Plugs and cords

■ **TIME:** About ½ hour to replace a plug
■ **SKILLS:** Stripping, tying, and wrapping wire
■ **TOOLS:** Wire stripper, needle-nose pliers, screwdriver

Faulty plugs pose the most common shock and fire hazards in a house. Plugs get stepped on, bumped, and yanked out by their cords. It's a good idea to regularly inspect your plugs—especially old ones—for loose connections, damaged wire insulation, and bent prongs that are in danger of breaking.

Replacing a faulty plug will make your home safer, and the job is easy. Buy a plug that has the same number of prongs as the one you're replacing.

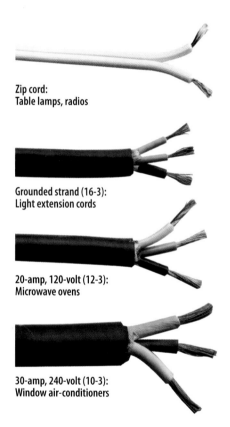

Zip cord:
Table lamps, radios

Grounded strand (16-3):
Light extension cords

20-amp, 120-volt (12-3):
Microwave ovens

30-amp, 240-volt (10-3):
Window air-conditioners

Types of cords

Cords have stranded, not solid, wire for flexibility. Zip cord, so called because the two wires can be easily zipped apart, is for light-duty appliances and lamps. Use cords with 16-gauge wire for appliances that draw 15 amps or less and 12-gauge wire for 20-amp appliances. For 240-volt appliances use wire that is 10-gauge or thicker.

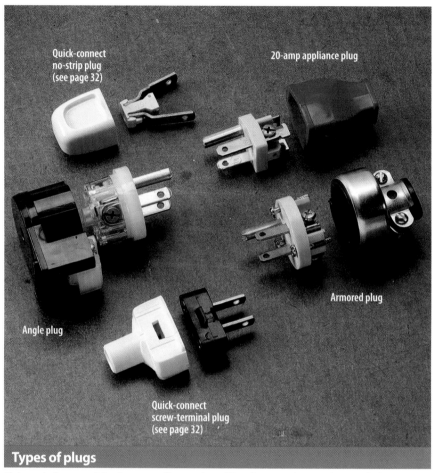

Quick-connect no-strip plug (see page 32)

20-amp appliance plug

Angle plug

Armored plug

Quick-connect screw-terminal plug (see page 32)

Types of plugs

Flat-cord plugs work for lamps, radios, and other low-amperage devices. Plugs rated for higher amperage accept thick cords and are often used for appliances such as irons. Armored plugs are used where the plug could be susceptible to damage, as on shop equipment.

Most lamp and extension cord plugs are polarized, with one wide blade (see page 7). Grounded plugs have a third, round prong for grounding; the two flat prongs are polarized.

Plugs for 240-volt appliances are available in several configurations.

MAINTAINING AND INSPECTING PLUGS

Electrical plugs carry just as much current as the wiring. They deserve to be treated with respect.

Never remove the grounding prong from an appliance plug. The grounding prong may protect you from shock, especially if the appliance gets wet.

Remove a plug from a receptacle by grasping the plug and pulling straight out. Pulling on the cord may loosen the connections, and pulling at an angle could bend the plug prongs.

If plug prongs do get bent, you can bend them back, but only a few times. Continual bending will cause a prong to eventually break. If a prong is made of two strips of metal and the strips come apart from each other, you may be able to bend them back together, but it is better to replace the plug.

Replacing a round-cord plug

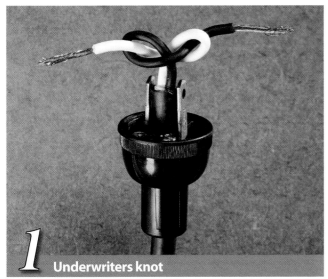

1 Underwriters knot

Snip off the old plug. Slide the cord through the body of the replacement plug. Strip off 3 inches of outer insulation and about ½ inch of wire insulation. Tie an Underwriters knot as shown.

2 Bend hooks and connect the wires

Pull the cord back so the knot is tight to the plug. Twist the wire strands tight with your fingers. Use a pair of needle-nose pliers to shape clockwise hooks to wrap around the screws.

Hook the wires on the screw shanks (attach the black wire to the brass screw) and tighten. Tuck in any stray strands. Make sure all wires and strands are neatly inside the plug. Slip on the cardboard cover.

Replacing an armored plug

1 Slide the plug onto the cord

An armored plug such as the 250-volt, 15-amp plug shown above has a steel clamp that grips the cord, so you don't have to tie an Underwriters knot. Slide the plug onto the cord and strip about ½ inch of insulation from the ends of the three wires. Twist the strands tight and use needle-nose pliers to form hooks.

2 Attach the wires

Attach the black and white wires to the hot terminals and the green wire to the ground terminal. When there is a silver-color hot terminal, the white wire goes to it. Tuck in loose wire strands as you tighten the screws. Tighten the cord clamp, slip on the plug cover, and tighten the screws.

Lamp plugs

- **TIME:** About 5 minutes to install a quick-connect plug; 15 minutes for a plug with screw terminals
- **SKILLS:** No special skill required for the quick-connect plug; stripping wire and making connections for the screw-terminal plug
- **TOOLS:** Knife or scissors for the quick-connect plug; wire stripper, needle-nose pliers, and screwdriver for the screw-terminal plug

Keep a few quick-connect plugs on hand and you'll be less tempted to put off replacing a faulty or questionable lamp plug. Installing one is only slightly more difficult and time-consuming than changing a lightbulb.

Lamps often have cord switches, which can fail. Installing or replacing a cord switch is a simple job. Some switches require wire stripping; others simply pierce the wire insulation to make contact.

INSTALLING A SCREW-TERMINAL CORD SWITCH

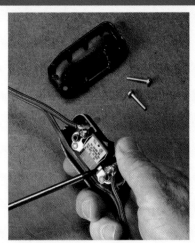

To install a screw-terminal cord switch, separate the wires and cut and strip the ends of the hot wire. Strip ¾ inch of insulation from each cut wire end and twist the bare wires tight. Thread the neutral wire through the bottom channel. Connect the stripped wire ends to the terminals, tighten the terminal screws, and replace the cover.

Wiring a quick-connect plug

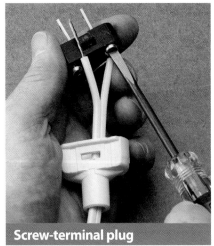

Screw-terminal plug

Cut the cord near the old plug. Separate the cord's two wires and strip ¾ inch of insulation from each wire. Slide the plug cover onto the cord. Twist each wire tight with your fingers, bend it into a hook shape, and firmly attach it to the terminal. Make sure the attachments are firm and remove any loose strands, then slide the plug body up and snap it in place.

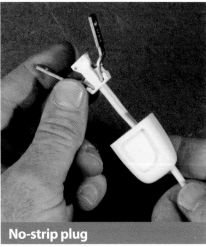

No-strip plug

This is the easiest plug to attach. Cut the cord and do not separate or strip the wires. Slide the plug cover onto the cord. Gently pull apart the plug's prongs and poke the cord into the hole at the bottom. Squeeze the prongs together and slide the cover up until it snaps into place.

Installing a no-strip cord switch

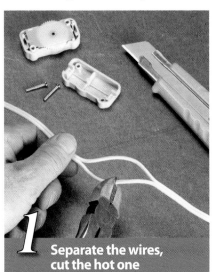

1 Separate the wires, cut the hot one

To install this kind of switch, carefully slice through the cord covering between the two wires and separate the wires for about 1½ inches. Snip only the hot (smooth) wire in the middle.

2 Lay the wires in the switch shell

Thread the neutral (ribbed) wire through the straight channel. Place the two cut ends of the hot wire into the split channel, as shown. Push the wires firmly into place. Replace the cover and tighten the screw.

Lamp sockets

■ **TIME:** About 1 hour to replace a lamp socket
■ **SKILLS:** Stripping wire, connecting wire to screws
■ **TOOLS:** Wire stripper, screwdriver, needle-nose pliers

Most floor and table lamps consist of a body, a base, a harp to support the shade, and a socket, which holds the lightbulb. The cord usually runs through a hollow threaded rod from the base to the socket.

When a lamp won't work and you know the bulb is OK, check the cord for damage. If the insulation is worn and cracked, replace the entire cord (see below). If the cord is OK, the problem is most likely in the socket.

Most lamps have felt bases that must be removed before repairing the lamps. Remove the felt by paring it off with a utility knife. After the repair reapply the felt with white glue.

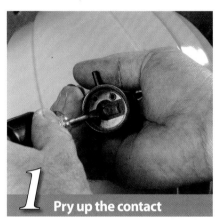

1 Pry up the contact

Unplug the lamp and remove the bulb. Remove the harp. Clean dust or debris out of the socket. Scrape rust off the center contact with a flat screwdriver, then gently pry up the tab. If this does not solve the problem, go on to the next steps to replace the socket.

2 Remove the socket

Examine the socket shell and find the word "press" on the sides. Push hard at that point and pull the unit apart into the components shown. Remove the cord from the socket. Unscrew the socket base from the lamp.

3 Connect the new socket

Slip the new socket base onto the cord, and tie an Underwriters knot (see page 31). Strip about ½ inch of insulation from the wires, twist the strands tight, and form them into hooks with a pair of needle-nose pliers. Wrap the wires clockwise around the screw shanks and tighten the screws. Reassemble the cardboard insulation and the outer shell. Attach the new socket to the lamp.

Rewiring a lamp

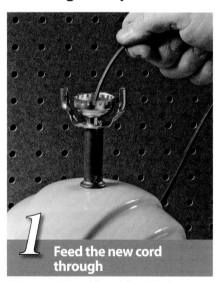

1 Feed the new cord through

Disconnect the old cord from the lamp socket and snip off the plug. Tie the new cord to the old one with a piece of string or some tape. Make the connection thin enough that it will slide through the center rod and pull the new cord through as you withdraw the old one.

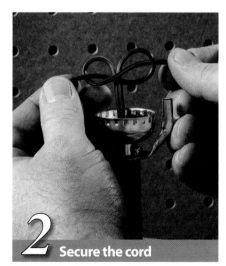

2 Secure the cord

Snip off the old cord and discard it. Tie an Underwriters knot (see page 31) in the new cord, leaving tag ends of about 2½ inches for each wire. Strip ½ inch of insulation from each wire. Connect the new cord to the socket as shown in step 3 above. Reassemble the lamp and attach a new plug to the cord (see pages 30–32).

LAMP SOCKET OPTIONS

Replacing a lamp socket can change the way your lamp turns on and off.
■ If the current socket has no switch, you can change to a switched socket—which most people prefer to, say, a cord switch.
■ You can choose a push-through switch, which turns on and off when you push it from one side or the other; a rotary switch, which turns on and off when you twist it; or a pull-chain switch.
■ You can also install a socket for a three-way bulb, allowing you to choose one of three light levels.

Switches

■ **TIME:** About ½ hour to test and replace a switch
■ **SKILLS:** Using testers (see instructions), connecting wires to screw terminals
■ **TOOLS:** Neon tester, continuity tester, screwdriver

S witches that are used often sometimes wear out. Unless the problem is a loose wire connection, you usually cannot repair a faulty switch; you'll have to replace it.

Testing and replacing switches is easy. If you want to replace your old switch with something more sophisticated—for example, a dimmer—check out the switch options on pages 50–51.

Testing switches

Use a neon tester...

Shut off the power, remove the cover plate and the screws holding the switch, and pull the switch out of the box. Turn the switch off and restore power to the circuit. Touch the probes of a neon tester to the switch's screw terminals. If the tester glows the circuit has power. Turn the switch on. Touch the probes to the terminals again. If the tester glows this time, the switch must be replaced.

Or a continuity tester

To test a switch using a continuity tester, **shut off the power** to the circuit leading to the switch and remove the switch from the box. Disconnect all the wires from the switch. Attach the tester clip to one of the terminals and touch the probe to the other. Flip the switch on. The tester will light up if the switch is good. The tester light should go off when you turn the switch off.

CAUTION

HANDLE WITH CARE
Hold only the metal flanges of the switch when pulling it out of a box. Be careful not to touch the terminal screws or to allow the screws to touch the edge of the box.

Test a three-way switch

To test a three-way switch, remove the switch and attach the clip to the common terminal (it's usually labeled on the switch body). Touch the probe to the other screw terminals; the tester should light when you touch one of them. Flip the switch; the tester should light when you touch the probe to the other terminal.

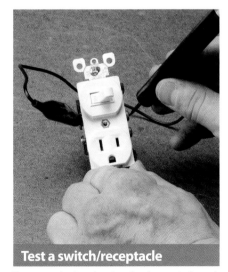

Test a switch/receptacle

To test a device that has both a switch and a receptacle, attach the continuity tester clip to one of the top (switch) terminals. Touch the probe to the top terminal on the other side. If the switch is working, the tester will light when the switch is on, and not light when it is off.

Replacing switches

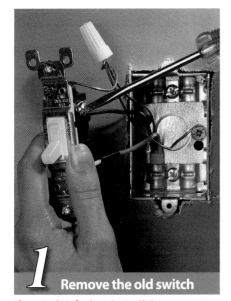

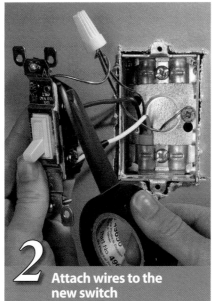

1 Remove the old switch

If a switch is faulty, **shut off the power** to the circuit, remove the screws holding the switch to the box, and gently pull out the device. Loosen the screw terminals and disconnect the wires. Snip off the wire ends, restrip them, and form new terminal loops if they are damaged.

2 Attach wires to the new switch

Inspect the wires in the box and wrap damaged insulation with electrical tape. Attach the wires to the terminals of the new switch and wrap electrical tape around the switch to cover the terminals, if your codes and inspector allow wrapping.

3 Reinstall the switch

Carefully tuck the wires and switch back into the box. Fasten the switch to the box by tightening the mounting screws. Don't force anything; switches crack easily.

Replacing a fixture-mounted switch

1 Remove the old switch and test the wiring

If a switch on a fixture or lamp does not work, **shut off power** to the fixture or unplug the lamp. Unscrew the nut holding the switch to the fixture and pull the switch out. Unscrew the wire nuts and remove the switch's wires, but do not disconnect the other wires from each other. To test a lamp's wiring, plug it in and touch the probes of a voltage tester to the wire ends, as shown. If the tester does not glow, rewire the lamp (see page 33).

2 Replace the switch

A fixture-mounted switch may operate via a pull chain, a toggle lever, a twist knob, or a push button. All four types fit into the same opening and are interchangeable. Use wire nuts to splice the wire ends of the new switch to the wire ends from the lamp. Insert the switch in the hole and tighten the nut.

Receptacles

■ **TIME:** About 5 minutes to test and 15 minutes to replace a receptacle
■ **SKILLS:** Using a tester (see instructions), connecting wires to terminals
■ **TOOLS:** Neon tester, wire stripper, receptacle analyzer, screwdriver

Damage to receptacles is not always readily apparent. Small cracks can lead to a short, and worn-out receptacles may not grip plug blades firmly. Receptacles are inexpensive and easy to replace, however, so you can change one for any reason, even if it is just old and worn or the wrong color. If you decide to replace a receptacle with one of a different type—for example, replace an ungrounded receptacle with a grounded one— read pages 7 and 52 first.

Testing receptacles

1 Test to see if the receptacle is live

With the power to the circuit on, insert one probe of a voltage tester into each slot of the receptacle. Do not touch the metal probes; only touch the insulated wires of the tester. If the tester glows the receptacle is working. Test both plugs of a duplex receptacle.

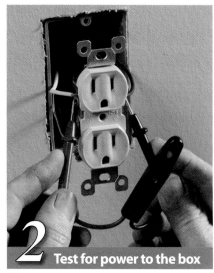

2 Test for power to the box

If the receptacle is not live, check its power source. Shut off the power to the outlet at the service panel, remove the cover plate, disconnect the screws holding the receptacle to the box, and pull out the receptacle. Restore power and touch one probe of the voltage tester to a brass screw terminal and the other to a silver colored terminal. The tester will light if the receptacle has power.

Replacing receptacles

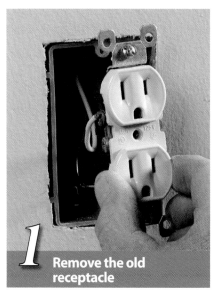

1 Remove the old receptacle

Shut off the power to the circuit at the service panel. Note which wires are attached to which terminals. Make notations on pieces of tape and wrap them on the wires if necessary. Loosen the terminal screws and disconnect the wires.

2 Wire the new receptacle

Inspect the wires in the box and wrap electrical tape around any damaged insulation. Snip off damaged wire ends, restrip, and make terminal loops. Attach the wires to the receptacle, positioning each loop clockwise on the terminal screw. Tighten the terminal screws.

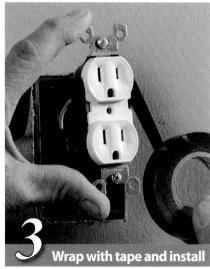

3 Wrap with tape and install

Wrap the body of the receptacle with electrical tape to cover the terminals if local codes permit. Carefully tuck the wires and the receptacle into the box and tighten the mounting screws. Don't force the receptacle into place—it may crack.

Testing grounding and polarization

Test a three-slot receptacle

Do not turn off the power. Insert one prong of a voltage tester into the short (hot) slot and the other into the grounding hole. The tester will glow if the receptacle is grounded and the slots are polarized. If the tester doesn't glow, put one probe in the grounding hole and the other in the long slot. A glow this time means the hot and neutral wires are reversed. If the tester doesn't glow in either test, the receptacle isn't grounded.

Test a two-slot receptacle

With the power on insert one probe of a voltage tester into the short (hot) slot and touch the other probe to the cover plate screw (above). The screw head must be clean and paint-free. Or remove the cover plate and insert one probe in the short slot and touch the other to the metal box (above right). If the neon tester glows, the box is grounded, and you can install a grounded three-hole receptacle.

If the tester doesn't glow, insert one prong into the long (neutral) slot and touch the other to the cover-plate screw or the box. A glowing tester means the box is grounded, but the receptacle is not correctly polarized; the hot and neutral wires are reversed. If the tester doesn't glow in either test, the box is not grounded, so it is not safe to install a three-hole receptacle in this location.

USING A RECEPTACLE ANALYZER

With this handy device you can test for power, grounding, and polarization almost instantly.

Leave the power on but unplug all equipment and turn off all the switches in the circuit of the receptacle you will be testing. Plug in the analyzer. A combination of glowing lights will tell you the status of the receptacle. The code for the lights is on the tester (far right).

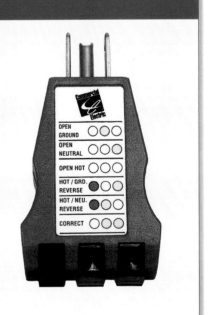

Thermostats

- **TIME:** About 1 hour for most inspections and repairs
- **SKILLS:** No special skills needed
- **TOOLS:** Screwdriver, artist's brush, short piece of wire, voltmeter or multitester, neon tester

A thermostat is a switch that senses temperature and turns your heater or air-conditioner on and off. Most homes have low-voltage units like the one described here. A transformer reduces power from 120 volts to around 24 volts and sends it to the thermostat. Some systems have two transformers, one for heating and one for air-conditioning.

Some HVAC systems have line-voltage thermostats. Be sure you know whether your thermostat is low-voltage or line-voltage. Turn off the power to a line-voltage thermostat before you remove the cover.

Possible causes of thermostat problems include faulty wiring, corroded thermostat contacts, and a defective transformer.

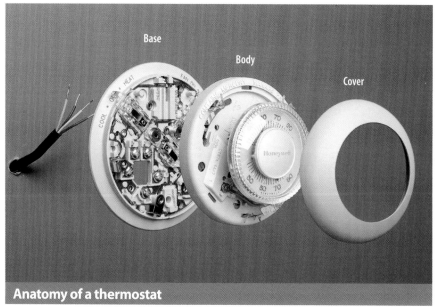

Anatomy of a thermostat

A low-voltage system begins with a transformer either mounted to a panel on the furnace or connected to an electrical box. Anywhere from two to six thin wires (depending on how many items are being controlled) lead to the thermostat base, where they are connected to terminals.

The thermostat body contains the heat-sensing device and the control dial. Because the voltage is so low, it is not necessary to shut off power to the thermostat while working on it—unless you are working on the transformer.

Cover plate removed

1 Clean the thermostat

Dust can cause a thermostat to malfunction. Remove the cover plate and brush out the thermostat with an artist's brush. Pay special attention to dust and dirt on contacts.

2 Remove the body

Remove the screws that hold the thermostat body to the base and pull the body away. Check to see that the base is fastened to the wall. If it is loose the thermostat could tilt, possibly affecting the settings. Blow on the body to remove more dust but do not handle the parts inside—they are sensitive.

3 Inspect the base connections

Look for loose, corroded, or broken wires coming into the base. If any are damaged, clip them, strip insulation from the ends, and reattach them. Check the terminal screws to ensure connections are secure.

Terminals will be marked with letters as shown.

Though marked "Y" a blue wire usually is attached here.

G

R

W   Y

4 Hot-wire the terminals

Cut a short piece of wire and strip insulation from both ends. Use it to jump between terminals. Touch one end to the R terminal and one to W, and the furnace burner should come on. Touch Y and G, and the fan should come on. If they do not, the thermostat may be faulty.

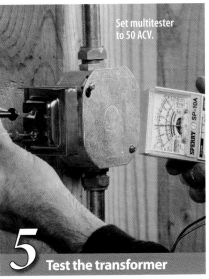

Set multitester to 50 ACV.

5 Test the transformer

Touch one probe of a voltmeter or multitester to each of the low-voltage terminals on the transformer. Set the dial to 50 ACV. If the meter does not detect current, the transformer is defective and needs to be replaced. If the meter does show power, the thermostat or wiring to it is defective.

6 Check power to the transformer

Before you buy a new transformer or thermostat, open the transformer box and make sure power is reaching the transformer. Touch one probe of a neon tester to the hot wires and the other to the box (if grounded) or the neutral wires.

INSTALLING A PROGRAMMABLE THERMOSTAT

A programmable thermostat automatically changes the temperature setting in your home for sleeping and waking hours. It also can deliver different temperatures when you're away.

There are many options to choose from. Some control heat only, while others also control air-conditioning. Some can be completely programmed in one sitting; others require a week-long run-through.

When shopping for a new thermostat, know the brand name and model number of your old thermostat

9811

and the heating and air-conditioning units to make sure the new thermostat is compatible. See the general steps for replacing a thermostat (right) but always follow the manufacturer's instructions that come with the unit.

REPLACING A THERMOSTAT

Label the wires as you disconnect them from the old thermostat. Take off the old thermostat. Pull the wires through the new wall plate and mount the plate securely to the wall. Check that it is level. Push any excess wire back into the wall and hook up the wires according to the manufacturer's instructions.

Attach the body to the cover plate. Set the clock and program the unit according to the manufacturer's instructions. Attach the cover.

Doorbells

- **TIME:** You may find and solve the problem in minutes or it could take several hours
- **SKILLS:** Using a continuity tester, perhaps a multitester
- **TOOLS:** Screwdriver, short piece of wire, continuity tester, voltmeter or multitester

A doorbell system incorporates a transformer, which reduces 120-volt line current to between 6 and 30 volts. Light-gauge wire (bell wire) connects the low-voltage side of the transformer to the bell, chime, or buzzer and a doorbell button in a circuit. Pressing the button, which is a spring-loaded switch, closes the circuit and activates the bell, chime, or buzzer.

If your bell does not work, find the cause by using the process of elimination described in the steps below. A voltmeter or multitester will make the job easier, but you also can do most tests with a short piece of bell wire or a screwdriver.

Unless you are working on the connections on the line-voltage side of the transformer, there's no need to shut off the power while inspecting a doorbell. The low voltage and low current from the transformer output is not hazardous. You can safely disconnect the bell-circuit wires from the output side of the transformer with the power still on.

Single-button system

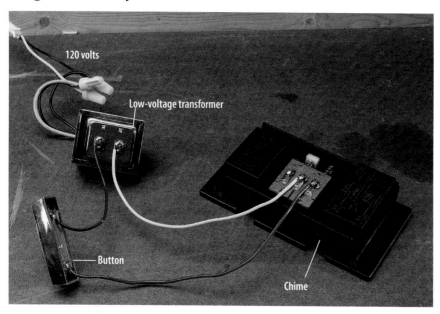

Two-button system

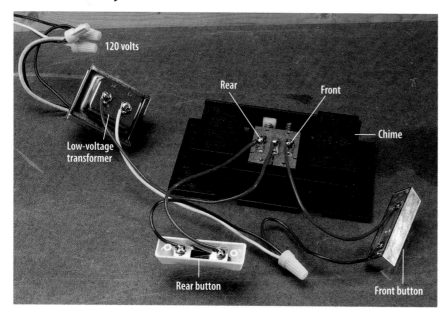

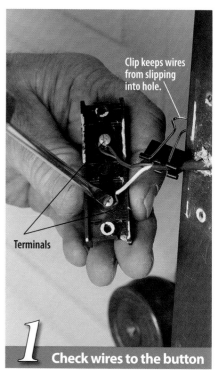

1 Check wires to the button

To check a doorbell system, remove the button, turn it over, and examine the connections. To make sure that the wires cannot accidentally slip back through the hole, attach a spring clip. Scrape away any corrosion on the terminals. Tighten the connections to the terminals. Wrap any faulty insulation with electrical tape.

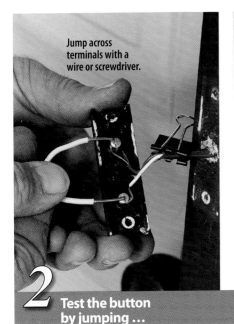

2 Test the button by jumping …

Weather and abuse make buttons the most vulnerable parts of a bell system. Test a button by jumping its terminals with a short piece of bell wire, as shown. If the bell sounds the button is faulty and should be replaced.

Jump across terminals with a wire or screwdriver.

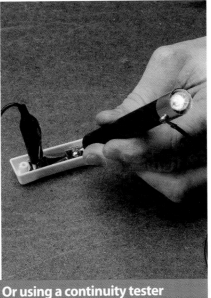

Or using a continuity tester

You can also test the button by disconnecting the wires and touching both terminals with a continuity tester. If the tester glows when the button is pressed, the button is working. If the bell still doesn't sound, disconnect the button, twist its wires together, and test further.

3 Check wires to the transformer

Find your transformer. It may be near your home's service panel or attached to a junction box in the vicinity of the door or the bell. Look for corrosion, loose wires, or faulty insulation.

Transformer

Disconnect wires for this test.

Set dial to 50 ACV or less.

4 Test the transformer…

To check the transformer, disconnect both wires and touch each terminal with the probes of a voltmeter or multitester. Set the dial at 50 ACV. If the meter shows no current at all, the transformer is the culprit and should be replaced. You also can test a transformer by jumping the low-voltage terminals with a screwdriver. If you see a weak spark, it is OK.

And replace if necessary

Shut off the power. Take the cover plate off the electrical box, remove the transformer, and disconnect the wires. Wire the new transformer just like the old one and reassemble the bell.

Doorbells *(continued)*

If the button, transformer, and chimes check out, then the trouble is probably a broken wire. Disconnect wires going into the bell, and test the current flow with a voltmeter or multitester. Or touch the front and rear wires to the transformer wire, and look for a spark.

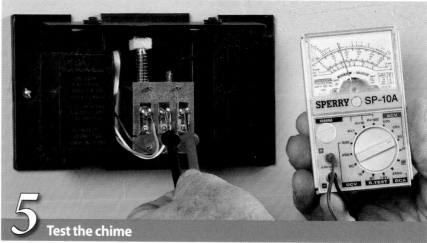

5 Test the chime

If the button, the wires, and the transformer are not to blame, check the bell. Remove the cover. Look for loose or broken connections. Even if you don't have a second button, the chime will have terminals labeled front and rear. Touch the voltmeter or multitester probes to the front and trans (meaning "transformer") terminals. If the meter registers a reading, power is going to the bell; the bell is defective. If you have a rear button, test again, touching the rear and trans terminals.

If you don't have a voltmeter, test the bell by removing it and temporarily wiring it directly to the transformer. If it is working it will ring.

Replacing chime units

When shopping for a doorbell, consider your wall: Will the new unit cover up the discolored area left by the old one, or will it require you to do some touch-up painting? Also make sure the doorbell or chime unit you choose has the same voltage rating as your home's transformer.

INSTALL A WIRELESS CHIME

Running new wires is a time consuming job. If you find damaged wiring, consider installing a wireless doorbell. This will cost more than a regular unit, but it saves you the trouble of running wires.

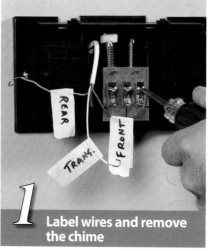

1 Label wires and remove the chime

You can shut off power to the circuit, but it's not necessary because the voltage is so low. The terminals are labeled, so mark the wires accordingly as you disconnect them. These labels also will prevent the wires from accidentally slipping through the hole and into the wall. Unscrew the chime from the wall and remove it.

2 Install the new chime

Attach the new chime to the wall with mounting screws. Use plastic anchors if you cannot drive a screw into a stud. Connect the low-voltage wires to the terminals and attach the cover.

TOOLS AND MATERIALS

Essential tools

Y ou don't need an arsenal of expensive tools for the
projects in this book. The basic tool kit shown on these
pages will be adequate for most repairs and installations.

Always buy good-quality tools and testers for durability
and accuracy.

Combination stripper
Use this tool instead of wire cutters to strip wires without
damaging them. It can also cut wire and bend it into loops.
Buy one that has a self-opening spring as shown; without it
stripping is much more laborious.

Multilevel tester
This device tests standard 120- and 240-volt circuits as well as
low-voltage wiring, such as door chimes or thermostats.

Continuity tester
A **continuity tester** quickly tells you when a circuit or device
is open or closed.

Needle-nose pliers
Use **needle-nose pliers** to bend wires into the loops required
when connecting to terminals.

Lineman's pliers
This basic electrician's tool has flat-face jaws that grab wires
firmly so you can neatly twist them together for a solid splice.
It also cuts wires.

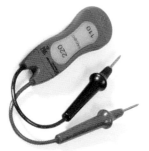

Neon voltage tester
Always test to determine when power is present. This neon
tester is the simplest tester.

Receptacle analyzer
Plug this tester into a receptacle and it will indicate whether power is present and whether grounding and polarization are correct.

Side-cutting pliers
Also called diagonal cutters, this tool makes it easy to snip wires in tight places and is ideal for snipping sheathing from cable.

Rotary screwdriver
Crank this screwdriver around to quickly drive or remove the little machine screws that attach devices and cover plates.

Utility knife
A utility knife is handy for stripping NM cable sheathing, cutting tape, and other wiring and repair chores.

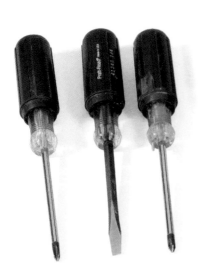

Screwdrivers
Screwdrivers designed for electrical work have insulating rubber grips that protect against shock. Buy sizes #1 and #2 of both straight and phillips types.

Voltage tester
This solenoid-type tester indicates voltage and polarity for a range of AC and DC voltages.

Specialized tools

If you will be running new cable or tackling other advanced projects, these tools are invaluable. Whenever a special tool would make the job go more smoothly, it is almost always a good idea to buy, rent, or borrow it.

Armored-cable cutter
If you are running armored cable or BX cable, use this tool to cut the metal housing.

Conduit bender
Make offsets and curves in rigid metal conduit with this tool. Trying to bend conduit without one usually results in kinks and wrinkles that make it hard to pull wire through the conduit.

Conduit reamer
This is the quickest and most effective tool for deburring conduit ends after cutting.

Drywall saw
This is the best tool for cutting into finished walls or ceilings. (A power saw, such as a reciprocating saw, will cut more easily, but you might not notice if you run into a hidden cable or pipe.)

Electric drill or cordless drill/driver
Running cable usually means drilling lots of holes, so you'll need a high-quality drill and a good collection of bits.

Fish tape
This is essential for running cable through finished walls and ceilings or for pulling wires through conduit. In some cases you'll need two of them.

Fishing drill bit
A fishing drill bit can drill holes and then pull cable through studs or joists, eliminating the need to cut holes in the wall or ceiling.

Flat pry bar
This style of pry bar will remove moldings with minimal damage.

Fuse puller
You can safely remove and install cartridge fuses with this insulated tool.

Hacksaw
Use a **hacksaw** to cut metal conduit or to nick armored sheathing prior to stripping.

Multitesters
Analog meter (left) or digital (right)
A multitester or multimeter measures AC and DC voltage, resistance, and current flow (volts, ohms, amperes). It also serves as a continuity tester. It comes in handy for troubleshooting and appliance repair.

Spade bit
Have several spade bits on hand because they burn out easily. To drill deep holes either use long bits or buy a bit extension.

Tubing cutter
You can cut rigid plastic or metal conduit with a plumbing tubing cutter. When you cut metal conduit with one, deburr the cut end so it will not nick the wire insulation.

Two-part circuit finder
A two-part circuit finder makes it easy to determine which circuit breaker controls a particular receptacle or (by using a screw-in adapter) light fixture.

Voltage detector
A noncontact voltage detector will help you determine whether wires running in walls are hot.

Wire and cable

Wire, cord, and cable (generically referred to as "conductors") are the pathways along which electricity travels. Wire is a solid strand of metal encased in insulation. Cord is a group of small strands surrounded by insulation. Cable is made of two or more wires wrapped in a protective sheathing of metal or plastic.

Most local codes allow you to use nonmetallic sheathed cable (NM cable) inside walls, floors, and other places where it can't be damaged and won't get wet. Information printed on the sheathing tells you what is inside. The top example, right, has two 14-gauge wires plus a bare ground wire, and is referred to as "14/2 G" cable ("G" for ground). Cable marked "14/3" has three wires plus a ground wire.

Armored cable contains wires wrapped in a flexible metal sheathing. Older armored cable, called BX, has a thin bonding wire but no actual ground wire; the sheathing itself is used to conduct the ground. Modern MC armored cable has a green-insulated ground wire.

Underground feed (UF) cable is watertight, with the sheathing molded around the wire. Many municipalities permit this for underground lines.

Different gauge wires carry different amounts of electricity—14-gauge carries a maximum of 15 amps, 12-gauge carries up to 20 amps, and 10-gauge wire handles up to 30 amps. Doorbells and other low-voltage circuits typically use 18-gauge wire.

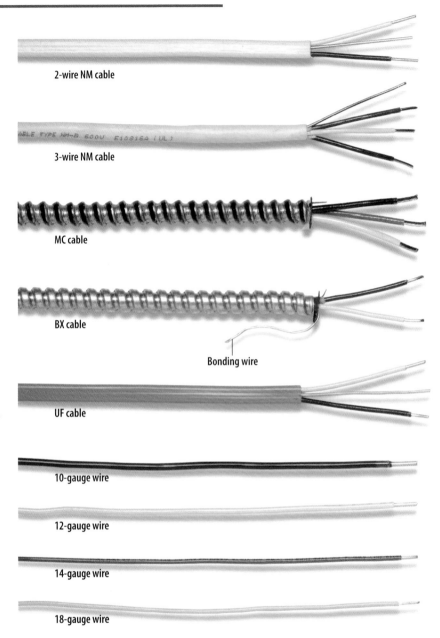

2-wire NM cable

3-wire NM cable

MC cable

BX cable

Bonding wire

UF cable

10-gauge wire

12-gauge wire

14-gauge wire

18-gauge wire

WHAT THE COLORS MEAN	
Color	**Function**
White	Neutral, carrying power back to the service panel
Black	Hot, carrying power from the service panel
Red and other colors	Also hot, color-coded to help identify which circuit they are on
White with black tape	A white wire that is being used as a hot wire
Bare or green	A ground wire

Conduit

Conduit is used to route wiring and protect the conductors from harm. It is most often installed in unfinished basements, garages, workshops, and similar places where the wiring is exposed and could be susceptible to damage.

EMT (electrical metallic tubing) is usually referred to as "thinwall." Available in diameters from ½ inch to 4 inches, thinwall is approved by most codes for exposed or concealed installations. It can be used in wet locations if all hardware is corrosion-resistant and connectors are rated as raintight. Thinwall can be buried in concrete with concrete-tight fittings.

Flexible metal conduit, or Greenfield, looks like armored cable without wires. Installation is much like armored cable (pages 76–77). Cut the pieces to length, feed the wires through, and install the completed pieces rather than pulling the wires after it's all installed.

Rigid nonmetallic conduit looks like plastic plumbing pipe and is essentially a plastic version of EMT. Fittings are joined to the conduit with solvent glue. It is approved for use in wet areas.

ENT (electrical nonmetallic tubing) is a flexible plastic conduit suitable for use in wet locations with approved fittings. It may not be exposed where physical damage is likely and cannot be exposed to the sun.

Liquid-tight flexible nonmetallic conduit is approved for wet or dry locations, including outdoors if the conduit is marked for that use.

On-surface wiring is ideal for remodeling projects when you don't want to break the wall or ceiling surface. The system uses raceway and matching boxes and fittings (pages 110–111).

Run individual conductors through conduit rather than cable. Individual wires are easier to pull and you can get more conductors into the conduit (see chart). Cable, designed to be installed in the open, could overheat inside conduit. Splices or other connections are not allowed inside any conduit; they must be inside boxes.

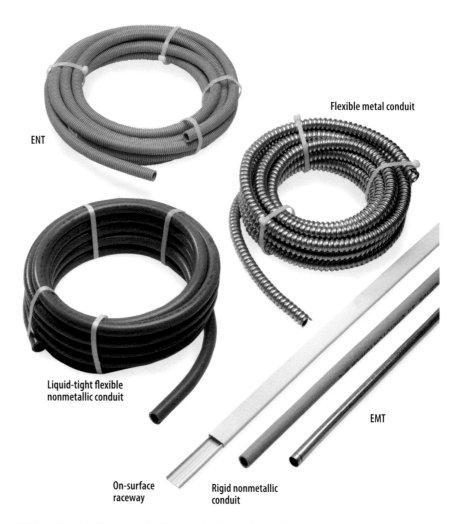

ENT

Flexible metal conduit

Liquid-tight flexible nonmetallic conduit

On-surface raceway

Rigid nonmetallic conduit

EMT

CONDUIT CAPACITY

Number of single insulated conductors (type THHN or THWN) of the wire gauge shown permitted in a conduit of the size shown

Wire	½" conduit	¾" conduit	1" conduit
14 gauge	13	24	39
12 gauge	10	18	29
10 gauge	6	11	18
8 gauge	3	5	9
6 gauge	1	4	6

Switches

Manufacturers offer a variety of switches. To begin with you have a choice of colors. The most readily available are brown, ivory, and white. But the differences extend far beyond appearance.

For most of your needs, you'll probably choose a **single-pole toggle,** which is available for a low price. "Toggle" simply refers to a switch with a lever that flips up and down.

Three-way and **four-way** switches control a light from two or three separate locations. To learn about wiring them, see pages 104–107.

If you want to add a switch without putting in a larger box, a **double** switch may be the solution. It fits into the same amount of space as a single switch.

A **rocker** switch functions the same way as a standard toggle switch and is slightly easier to use.

A **dimmer** switch allows you to adjust lighting levels to suit your needs. A sliding dimmer brightens the light as you slide it upward. The rotary type comes in two versions. One version turns lights on or off with a push; the light level changes by turning the knob. The other type dims the light by rotating the knob counterclockwise until it turns off.

LOOK FOR THE UL SYMBOL

The UL symbol means that electrical materials have been checked for any defects by Underwriters Laboratories, an independent testing organization. Local codes may prohibit using items not UL-listed.

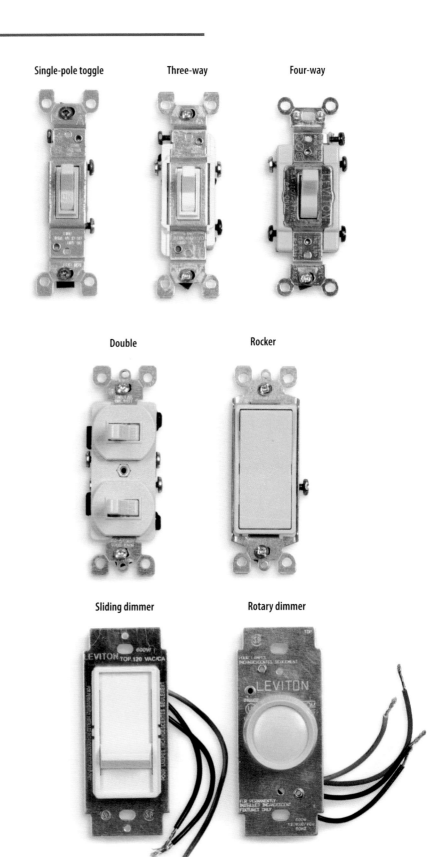

Single-pole toggle   Three-way   Four-way

Double   Rocker

Sliding dimmer   Rotary dimmer

Special switches

Of the many available switches built to suit special needs, the ones on this page are some of the most common. Take a trip to a home center or a lighting store and you may find the switch that does exactly what you want. To find out how to install these switches, see pages 84–85.

If you have power tools or other devices that you don't want children to play with, consider installing a tamperproof switch. Operated only with a key, it can be wired to control the receptacle connecting the equipment.

For security in your backyard, or to have a light automatically greet you as you approach your house, choose a **motion-sensor security** switch. Its wide-angle infrared beam detects motion and turns the light on automatically. With most units you can choose how long the light will stay on.

A **pilot-light** switch has a little bulb that glows when power flows through the switch. Use it when a fixture or appliance is out of sight. These switches often control closet lights, attic exhaust fans, basement lights, and garage lights.

If you need to squeeze both a switch and an outlet into a single box, use a **switch/receptacle**. Also use this switch to easily add a receptacle to a room. This switch can be wired so the receptacle is live all the time or wired so the switch controls the receptacle.

A **timer** turns a fixture on and off at preset times. A **programmable** switch can be programmed to turn a fixture on and off up several times a day. Either is useful to control lights for security and deterring burglars when you are away from home.

A **time-delay** switch can be set to leave a fixture on for up to 60 minutes. Use one for a vent fan, heat lamp, or light. Screw in a **socket receiver switch** to make a remote-control light, controlled by a **keychain remote.**

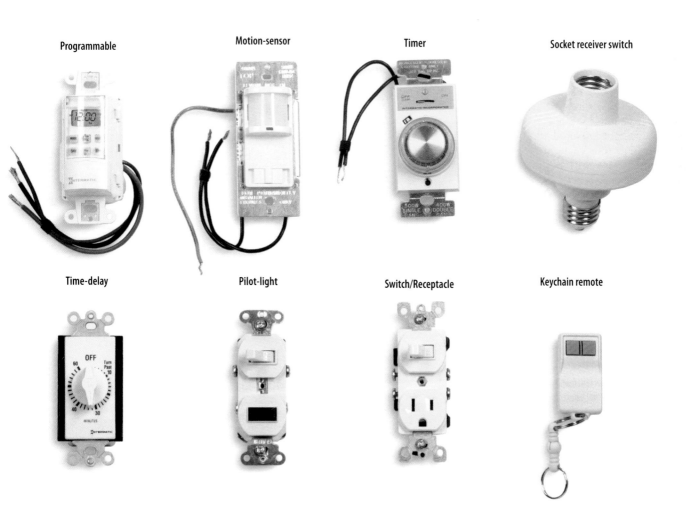

Programmable

Motion-sensor

Timer

Socket receiver switch

Time-delay

Pilot-light

Switch/Receptacle

Keychain remote

Receptacles

A standard duplex receptacle has two outlets for receiving plugs. Each outlet has a long (neutral) slot, a shorter (hot) slot, and a half-round grounding hole. This setup ensures that the plug will be polarized and grounded (see page 7).

Receptacles are rated for maximum current capacity. A **20-amp grounded** receptacle has a T-shape neutral slot; use it only on 20-amp circuits. For most purposes a **15-amp grounded** receptacle is sufficient. When replacing a receptacle in an ungrounded outlet box, install a **15-amp ungrounded** receptacle, intended only for use in older homes without ground wires in the circuits. Use a three-pronged plug adapter on an ungrounded receptacle only if the wall-plate screw is grounded (see page 37 for a way to test this). The switch in a combination **switch/receptacle** can be hooked up to control the receptacle. A 20-amp single grounded receptacle makes it nearly impossible to overload a critical circuit. For outdoors, in basements, or within 6 feet of a water fixture, install **ground fault circuit interrupter** (GFCI) receptacles (see page 87). Select a **240-volt** receptacle based on the appliance amperage rating. Plugs required for appliances of 15, 20, 30, and 50 amps will have different prong configurations.

CAUTION

REPLACE, DON'T CHANGE

Replace a receptacle with one that is just like the old one. Change types only if you are certain that the wiring is suitable. Do not replace an ungrounded outlet with a grounded one unless the box is grounded or you run a ground wire to it.

Essential receptacles

15-amp ungrounded

20-amp grounded

15-amp grounded

Switch/Receptacle

Specialized receptacles

GFCI receptacle

30-amp 120/240-volt wall-mounted

50-amp 120/240-volt

Duplex with 20-amp 240V for air conditioner

20-amp 120V grounded single

50-amp 120/240-volt grounded

Boxes

An electrical box's primary function is to house electrical connections. Those connections might be to a switch, a receptacle, the leads of a light fixture, or other sets of wires.

Electrical codes require that all wire connections or cable splices be inside an approved metal or plastic box. And every box must be accessible—you cannot bury it inside a wall. This protects your home from the danger of fire and makes it easier to inspect and upgrade your wiring in the future.

Codes govern how many connections you're allowed to make within a box, depending on its size. If you must make more connections, you have to use a larger box.

There are boxes to suit almost any depth of wall or ceiling, to support heavy fixtures such as ceiling fans, and for remodeling work and new construction. If, for instance, you'll be pulling cables through a finished wall, you can choose from a number of retrofit boxes that can be mounted with minimal damage to the wall.

Boxes for switches and receptacles serve as the workhorses in any electrical installation. Some of the metal ones can be ganged into double, triple, or larger multiples by removing one side and linking them together. Most codes accept switch/receptacle boxes made of plastic, but they can't be ganged. If you are using conduit, Greenfield, or BX, you must use metal boxes to ground the system.

Utility boxes are surface-mounted in basements and garages to hold switches or receptacles. Boxes for fixtures or junctions may support lighting fixtures or split circuits into separate branches.

CHOOSING THE CORRECT BOX SIZE

Type of box	Size in inches (height × width × depth)	Maximum number of wires allowed in box		
		14-gauge	12-gauge	10-gauge
Switch/ Receptacle	3×2×1½	3	3	3
	3×2×2	5	4	4
	3×2×2¼	5	4	4
	3×2×2½	6	5	5
	3×2×2¾	7	6	5
	3×2×3½	9	8	7
Utility	4×2⅛×1½	5	4	4
	4×2⅛×1⅞	6	5	5
	4×2⅛×2⅛	7	6	5
Fixture/ Junction	4×1¼ round or octagonal	6	5	5
	4×1½ round or octagonal	7	6	6
	4×2⅛ round or octagonal	10	9	8
	4×1¼ square	9	8	7
	4×1½ square	10	9	8
	4×2⅛ square	15	13	12
	4¹¹⁄₁₆×1½ square	14	13	11
	4¹¹⁄₁₆×2⅛ square	21	18	16

BOX CAPACITY

Overcrowd a box and you risk damaging wire connectors, piercing insulation, and cracking a switch or receptacle, any of which could cause a short. That is why codes spell out how many wires you can install in a box.

The chart above gives standard requirements. Other items may add to the total number of wires a box can hold. As you count wires keep in mind these rules:

- Don't count fixture leads (the wires that are connected to the fixture).
- Count a wire that enters and leaves without a splice as one.
- Count each cable clamp, stud, or hickey inside the box as one wire.
- Count each receptacle or switch as one.
- Count grounding wires entering a box as one but do not count grounding wires that begin and end in the box.

New-work switch/receptacle boxes

These boxes are designed for quick installation when the framing is exposed. They all have built-in gauges to make it easy to install them flush with the surface of the finished wall.

4×4 box with nailing spurs

Metal box with nailing bracket. Side removes so additional box can be added on

2×4 box with front-nailing bracket

Side W-bracket holds box away from the stud.

2×4 plastic box with front-nailing bracket

2×4 plastic box with 16d nails

4×4 plastic box with nails angled for easy fastening

Retrofit switch/receptacle boxes

When installing new electrical service where the walls are finished, use boxes designed to minimize damage to the wall. If the special clips do not work, you may be able to attach the boxes to framing pieces with screws driven through holes inside the boxes.

Metal wings slip behind wall; flaps fold over the box.

Tightening the screw pulls the pointed flanges forward.

Screw-in clamps move forward to hold box in place.

A 2×4 plastic box with plastic "ears" that swing out and forward as screws tighten

A 4×4 plastic box with plastic ears

New-work fixture/junction boxes

New-work wiring refers to work done on a freshly framed wall. With no drywall or plaster in the way, it is easy to install ceiling fixture boxes that are solid enough to hold a heavy chandelier or a fan. Remember that all junction boxes must remain accessible—never cover them with drywall.

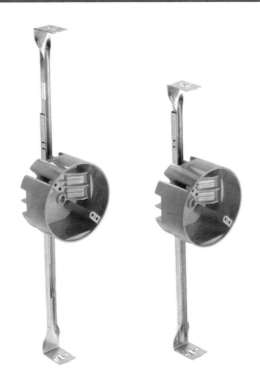

Metal octagonal box requires framing behind it if it will support a heavy fixture.

Round plastic fixture box has a bracket with sharp points so you can quickly tap it in place, then secure it with screws.

Telescoping brackets allow you to position these boxes anywhere between joists.

Octagonal junction box with side bracket nailed to framing.

Retrofit fixture/junction boxes

Retrofitting and adding new wiring to old walls is challenging. Often it's not easy to secure a fixture box when there's drywall or plaster in the way. For heavy ceiling fixtures use a brace bar that can be slipped into the hole and expanded from joist to joist (see page 113).

A shallow box like this is sometimes needed in older homes with plaster walls.

USE NEW INSTALLATION BOXES IN UNFINISHED SPACES

Most homes have areas where the walls or ceilings are unfinished, such as basements, attics, and garages. Whenever you are adding improvements to these areas or adding junction boxes that will serve existing circuits, use new installation boxes. Use metal boxes with metal cover plates, even if you are using nonmetallic sheathed cable, because they may get bumped. Plastic boxes will crack.

Wings come forward as you tighten the screws, clasping the box to the plaster or drywall.

Most retrofitting starts with standard junction boxes located in accessible areas.

Specialized boxes

Wiring can be full of surprises. If you run into an unusual situation, you can probably find a specialized box that can help. Here are a few of the boxes designed to cope with tight spaces, new framing materials, and changes in wall thickness.

A weatherproof die-cast aluminum box can be surface-mounted for outdoor fixtures.

Metal studs are becoming popular for house construction. This box mounts on either side of one.

This box mounts on the flat side of a metal stud.

A screw on the wall clip lets you adjust the depth of the box to account for the thickness of tile or paneling.

This 1¼-inch-thick box fits shallow wall cavities.

A ceiling box slips onto a joist and is strong enough to support a ceiling fan.

Box accessories

Box accessories are numerous. Some, such as mudrings, should be installed before applying the wall surface. Others attach to installed boxes for special needs.

Weatherproof cover plate for an exterior GFCI receptacle

Knockout filler plugs a knockout hole that is not being used.

Extender ring brings a fixture box out ½ inch—especially useful when drywall is added over plaster.

Blank plate and one- and two-device mudrings for placing receptacles in large boxes

Box extender slides inside the box.

Blank plate covers an octagonal or round junction box.

Weathertight housings for an outdoor box: blank, one-fixture, and two-fixture

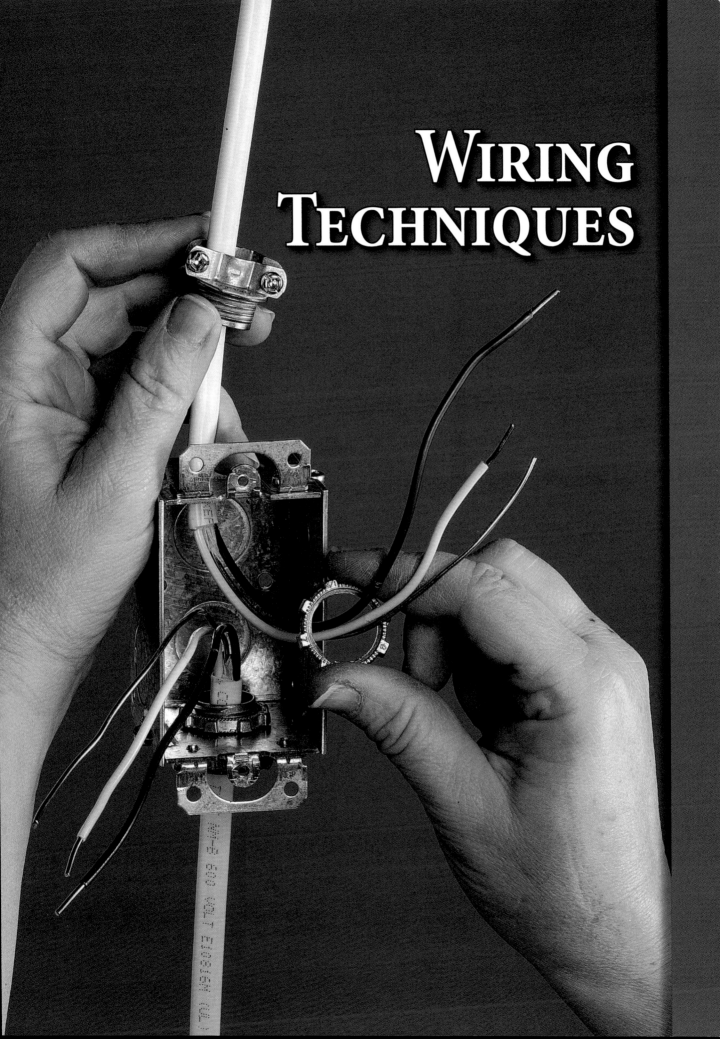

WIRING TECHNIQUES

Stripping and joining wire

- **TIME:** About 5 minutes or less
- **SKILLS:** Stripping wire
- **TOOLS:** Cable ripper, utility knife, side cutters, combination tool, lineman's pliers

Before making electrical connections you must remove some of the sheathing that encases the three or four wires of the cable. You will also need to strip some of the insulation that coats the individual wires. Stripping techniques are easy but exercise care when removing sheathing in order to avoid damaging any of the underlying insulation. Also be careful to strip the insulation without nicking the copper wire—this would weaken it.

Instead of stripping the wires after the cable is pulled into the box, strip the wires before inserting them. That way if you make a mistake you can cut off the damaged portion and try again.

CAUTION

STRIP WIRE CAREFULLY

This job is simple, but it must be done with great care or you could end up with dangerous electrical shorts. If you think you may have accidentally damaged some insulation, cut the cable back to a place behind the potentially dangerous spot and start again.

Another possible problem: If you cut into the copper wire while stripping the insulation, you can weaken the wire. This may cause it to break while you are making a connection later.

Stripping sheathing

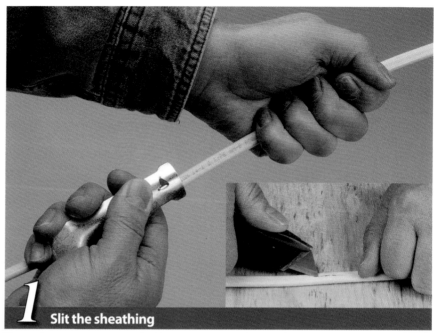

1 Slit the sheathing

The easiest way to remove plastic sheathing from nonmetallic sheathed cable is to use an inexpensive cable ripper. Slip 6 to 8 inches of cable into the ripper's jaws, squeeze, and pull. This slits open the sheathing without damaging the insulation of internal wires. The same job can be done with a utility knife, but you must be careful: Run the blade right down the middle so it doesn't strip insulation from the wires.

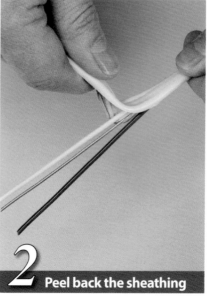

2 Peel back the sheathing

Pull back the sheathing you have just slit as well as the paper wrapping or strips of thin plastic, if any. You'll find two or three separately insulated wires, as well as a bare ground wire.

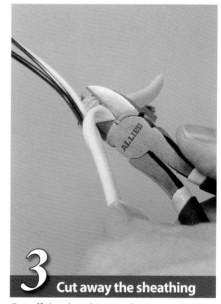

3 Cut away the sheathing

Cut off the sheathing and paper with a pair of side cutters. Or use a knife, taking care to point the blade away from the wires.

Stripping wire

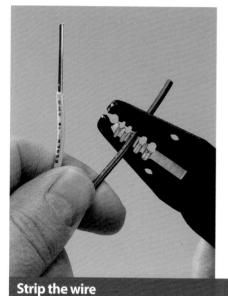
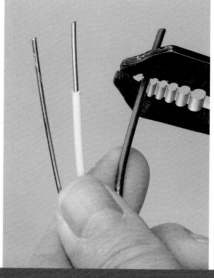
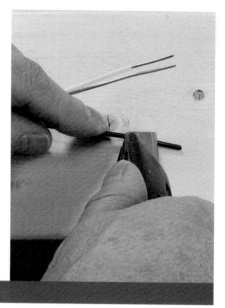

Strip the wire

You can strip insulation from wires with a combination tool, which has separate notches for the different sizes of wires. The wire size in gauge number is marked on the jaws. The tool also cuts wire.

The tool cuts the insulation but will not nick the wire when it is fully closed.

Place the wire in the correct notch, close the handles, turn the tool around the wire to score the insulation all around, and push the tool away from you.

Stripping also can be done with a utility knife, but be careful not to dig into the copper wire. Place the wire on a scrap piece of wood, hold the blade at a slight angle, and make several light slices into the insulation.

Joining wires

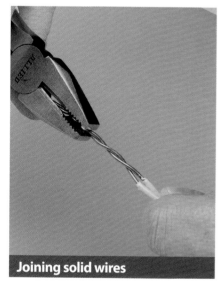

Joining solid wires

Join solid wires by using a pair of lineman's pliers. Cross the two wires, grab both wires with the pliers, and twist clockwise. Both wires should twist—do not twist one wire around the other. Turn for several revolutions but don't twist so tightly that the wires are in danger of breaking. Screw a wire connector onto the two wires (see page 60).

1 Join stranded to solid wires

Often a stranded wire (made of many thin wires) has to be spliced to a solid wire, as when hooking up a light fixture or dimmer switch. The stranded wire is more flexible, so the two won't twist together. Wrap the stranded wire around the solid wire.

2 Fold the solid wire over

Bend the solid wire so it clamps down on the stranded wire. Screw a wire connector onto the two wires and wrap the connection with electrician's tape.

Working with wire

The final—and most gratifying—phase of an electrical installation comes when you tie all those wires together and attach them to the switches, light fixtures, and receptacles. Don't take shortcuts with wire connections and splices. Cap splices with wire connectors and wrap tape around each connector. Make pigtails wherever they are needed instead of trying to connect two or more wires to a terminal. Finally don't overcrowd a box with too many wires (for limits see the chart on page 53).

HOW MANY WIRES IN A CONNECTOR?

Wire connector	12-gauge wires	14-gauge wires
Red	2-4	2-5
Yellow	2-3	2-4
Orange	2	2-4

Using wire connectors

To complete a splice of two or more wires, use wire connectors. These come in a variety of sizes. Select the size you need depending on how many wires you will connect as well as the thickness of the wires (see chart, left). Wire connectors firm up the splice and protect bare wires better than tape. First twist the wires firmly together. Do not depend on the connector to do the joining. Twist the wire connector on, turning it by hand until it tightens firmly. As a final precaution wrap the connector clockwise with electrician's tape, overlapping the wires.

Connecting wire to a terminal

1 Strip the insulation

Strip the insulation from just enough wire to make a loop that will wrap around the terminal—about ¾ inch.

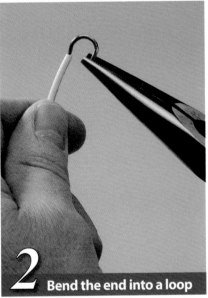

2 Bend the end into a loop

Form the wire into a loop using needle-nose pliers. It takes practice to make loops that lie flat under the terminal screw and are neither too big nor too small. Be sure wire insulation will not be trapped under the terminal screw when you connect the wire to the device.

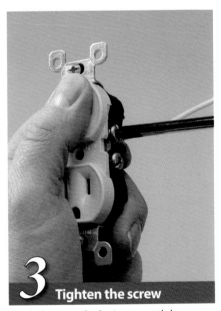

3 Tighten the screw

Hook the wire clockwise around the terminal so tightening the screw will close the loop. A black wire goes to the brass screw; a white wire attaches to the silver terminal. Tighten the screw but avoid overtightening, which can damage the device. If you crack a device, replace it.

Connecting wire

Attach to terminals

Attach multiple wires to a terminal with a pigtail

Never attach more than one wire to a terminal. Codes prohibit it, and it's unsafe because terminal screws are made to hold only one wire. The safe way to join multiple wires to a terminal is to cut a short piece of wire (about 4 inches), strip both ends, and splice it to the other wires as shown to form a pigtail.

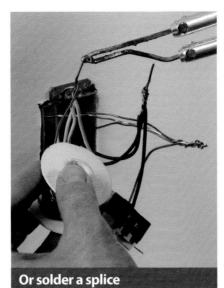

Or solder a splice

Make sure local codes permit soldered connections; some codes require soldered splices, but they are more often prohibited for house wiring. Twist wires together so that one extends 1 inch beyond the splice. Heat the wires with a soldering iron, then touch lead-free, rosin-core solder to the wires. The solder should melt into the splice. Tape the soldered splice.

BACKWIRED DEVICES

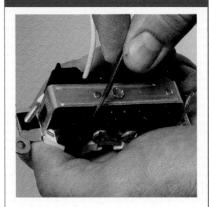

Many receptacles and switches have holes for wire connections in the back. However most professionals do not use them. Wires connected this way are simply not as secure as those screwed to a terminal. To make backwire connections strip the wire (a stripping gauge often is provided, showing you how much insulation to remove) and poke it into the correct hole. On a receptacle the holes are marked for white and black wires.

Grounding receptacles and switches

How you ground receptacles and switches depends on local codes as well as the type of box and cable. With older installations of flexible armored cable (BX), Greenfield, or metal conduit, the metal of the wiring casing and the metal of the box substitutes for the grounding wire. By attaching the device firmly to the box, you have grounded it. Modern codes, however, call for MC armored cable, which has a grounded wire (left photo, above),

or a separate ground wire for conduit or Greenfield. Ideally the ground wire should be attached to the box via a pigtail (middle photo). Use this technique with nonmetallic sheathed cable and metal boxes. In some older installations a ground wire is attached to a metal box using a clip that mounts to the side of the box (not shown). With nonmetallic boxes connect the ground wire directly to the device (right photo).

Installing boxes in unfinished space

■ **TIME:** About 3 hours for installing 10 boxes
■ **SKILLS:** Basic carpentry skills
■ **TOOLS:** Tape measure, hammer or drill with screwdriver bit

To wire a room with unfinished walls and ceiling, such as a basement remodeling or a room addition, you'll fasten boxes to the framing. When attaching the boxes be sure they protrude from the framing the same thickness as your drywall or paneling—usually ½ inch. Do not install any electrical box where it will be completely covered or otherwise inaccessible after the walls are finished.

This page shows some boxes for wall switches and receptacles.

The opposite page shows various types available for ceiling fixtures—some install from below, some install from above. These fasten to the joist with screws or nails. If there is a joist at the spot where you want a ceiling box, use a box with a hanger bracket or an L-bracket.

Nonmetallic handy box

Many boxes have a series of gauging notches on their sides. Determine the thickness of the drywall and/or paneling you will be installing and align the box to the appropriate notch as you attach it. A nail-up box like this one is the easiest to install.

Gangable boxes

These have detachable sides, so you can connect them together to form double- or triple-size boxes. To attach the boxes without using special mounting hardware, drive screws or nails through the holes and into the framing.

PLACING BOXES

In a typical room place switch boxes 48 to 50 inches above the floor and receptacles 12 to 16 inches above floor level. In most cases they must be placed so that no point along any wall is more than 6 feet from a receptacle. This means that you'll have to install at least one receptacle every 12 feet along the wall. For kitchens and bathrooms special requirements apply. See page 82 for common electrical code requirements.

L-bracket box

Some L-bracket boxes adjust to suit the thickness of your wall material. Others accommodate only one thickness. Hold the box in position against the framing and drive two nails or screws through the holes in the bracket.

Utility box

Use a utility box and conduit or armored cable in an area where you don't need a finished appearance. Attach boxes to masonry with anchors or masonry screws.

If you need to install a fixture box between joists, use a box with a bar hanger. Attach the ends of the brackets to the joists and slide the box into the desired position.

Some junction boxes come with brackets attached. Others have nails that drive into a joist, stud, or rafter.

Regardless of the type of box you're installing, always secure it with two fasteners. If the box will support a ceiling fan or other heavy fixture, make sure it's anchored securely to carry the load. If a box has been correctly mounted but still doesn't feel firm enough, add a framing piece and secure it to that as well.

Run the wires after you have installed the boxes. After you've roughed in the wiring, but before you install the switches and receptacles, put up the drywall on the walls and ceiling. Finish and prime the surfaces and install the devices.

Box with hanger bracket

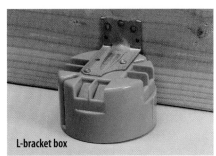

L-bracket box

Box with bar hanger

4-inch octagonal junction box

Square junction box

OVERHEAD LIGHT PLACEMENT

One pleasing way to light a room is with recessed lights (see pages 96–97) or small fixtures. To plan for a group of symmetrically placed lights, make a map of your ceiling and experiment by drawing circles, each representing the area lit by a recessed fixture.

When you experiment with your design, try to arrange the lights so they are half as far from the walls as they are from each other. A pleasingly symmetrical pattern usually results. Start by arranging lights 6 feet apart and 3 feet from the walls.

Avoid positioning them closer than 4 feet apart. Include any suspended or track lighting you need for task illumination or to accent an attractive area of the room.

Don't expect to achieve an arrangement that's perfectly symmetrical; few ceilings will allow for that. Also keep in mind that, with recessed lighting, you may not be able to put all the lights exactly where you want them because there will be joists in the way. In most cases a less-than-perfect arrangement will not be noticeable.

Installing boxes in finished space

■ **TIME:** About 30 minutes per box, not including running new wire
■ **SKILLS:** Basic carpentry skills
■ **TOOLS:** Drill, utility knife, keyhole saw, saber saw, screwdriver, hammer

Installing electrical work is a greater challenge when the walls and ceilings are finished. Often patching and painting can take far more time than the electrical work itself! Plan the placement so you avoid making unnecessary holes.

Avoid contact with the framing wherever possible. Using special boxes designed for installation in finished space, you often can make a hole the size of the box and secure the box to the wall or ceiling surface.

Before you begin plan how you're going to get cable to the new location (see pages 66–69).

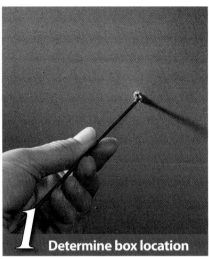

1 Determine box location

Drill a small hole in the wall. Insert a bent wire with a 6-inch leg and rotate it. If you hit something you've probably found a stud. Drill 6 inches to one side. If you strike wood again, you may have hit a fire block. Drill another hole 3 inches higher or lower. Keep trying until you can rotate the bent wire freely.

2 Trace around box

Some boxes come with a template that can be held against the surface and traced around. Otherwise use the box itself and center it on the hole you rotated the wire in. Make sure the template or box is plumb before you mark the outline.

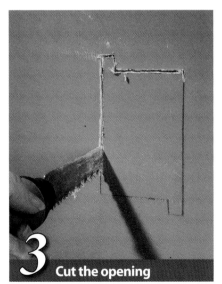

3 Cut the opening

Carefully cut around the traced outline. If the surface is drywall, use a utility knife. If you are cutting into plaster walls, use a keyhole saw. If the plaster is crumbly, mask the outline with tape. For a wood-surfaced wall, drill a 1/4-inch access hole in each corner and use a saber saw. Run cable (see pages 66–69).

4 Fasten with side clamps…

Side-clamp boxes grip the wall from behind when you tighten the screws. Pull 8 inches of cable through the box and insert the box into the wall. Hold the box plumb as you tighten the clamps. Alternate from side to side as you work so the box seats evenly. Avoid overtightening the clamps.

Or tighten wing clips

Loosen the screw centered in the receptacle box until the wing bracket is completely extended from the back. Hold the wings against the body of the box and push the box into the hole. Tighten the screw until the box is firmly in place.

Box attached to framing

Bar hanger

2×4 support

With access from above

A ceiling box supports a fixture, so it must be securely attached to the framing. If you are fortunate enough to have attic space above, the job can be done without damaging your ceiling. Mark the location of each box on the ceiling and drive nails as reference points. Cut the hole for the box. If there is a nearby joist, attach an L-bracket box directly to it. If not use a bar hanger or frame in a 2×4 support.

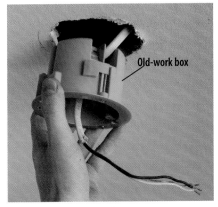

Old-work box

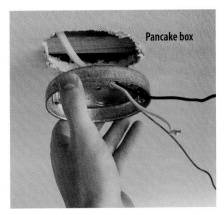

Pancake box

Bar hanger

With no access from above

If you cannot work from above, use one of these methods. For most light fixtures, which weigh less than 5 pounds, use an old-work box. Cut the hole, slip the box in, and tighten screws to clamp the box to the drywall or plaster. If a joist is in the way and you cannot move the box to the side, install a pancake box, which is screwed directly to the joist. To support a heavy fixture such as a chandelier or a fan, follow the instructions on pages 112–113 for installing a braced box. If the ceiling is damaged anyway, you may choose to cut out a rectangular section of ceiling and install a bar hanger box.

Repair the ceiling

After checking the electrical installation, patch the ceiling. With drywall you may be able to use the same piece you cut out. Nail the panel to the joists and tape the seam with joint compound. For a plaster ceiling fill with patching compound.

Running cable in finished space

■ **TIME:** About 3 hours
■ **SKILLS:** Drilling and patching
■ **TOOLS:** Power drill, ¾- and 1-inch bits, fish tape, keyhole saw, utility knife, chisel, hammer, standard carpentry tools

Do some detective work before you start running cable through finished walls and ceilings. As far as possible, determine what's in the wall or ceiling cavity. Look for access routes from an unfinished attic floor or basement ceiling. Check to see if there is insulation or blocking in the way. Determine whether or not there is a way to run cable parallel to the joists and studs. Make as few holes as possible because patching walls and ceilings is often the most time-consuming part of running cable. Repair holes you cut for access with patching plaster, drywall tape, and joint compound.

1 Drill top or bottom plates…

If there is access from above or below, drill into the top or bottom plates of the wall frame. For a double plate or awkward angle, use a bit extension. After drilling the hole fish the cable to the box opening. If you hit fire blocking (horizontal pieces between the studs), see step 4.

Or cut an opening

When there is no room for drilling through the plates from above or below, bore from the side instead. At the top of the wall, cut an opening to expose the single or double plate. At the bottom there will only be a single plate; remove the baseboard and make the cutout ¾ inch above the floor.

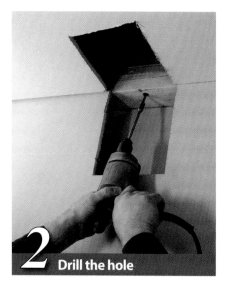

2 Drill the hole

Using a bit extension bore into the bottom of the plate, angling toward the center. Bore slowly to avoid overheating the bit and the drill. If you encounter nails you may have to drill in a different direction. Remember to wear goggles when drilling.

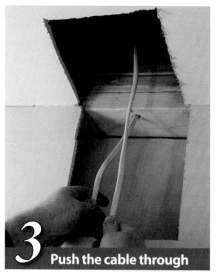

3 Push the cable through

Push the cable up or down to the box opening. Then loop it through the plate. Pulling cable through walls is a job for two people. One person tugs—not too hard or the sheathing might tear—from the attic or basement. The other coils cable and feeds it through the opening, taking care to avoid kinks and knots.

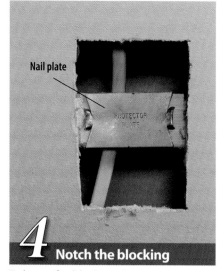

Nail plate

4 Notch the blocking

To locate fire blocking slip a tape measure through the hole and push it until it strikes the blocking. Measure to that point and make an opening that straddles the blocking. Chisel a notch that is large enough to accommodate the cable easily. After you've run the cable, but before you patch the hole, install a nail plate.

Short runs of cable

- **TIME:** About 2 hours, not including wall patching
- **SKILLS:** Pulling wire and patching drywall or plaster
- **TOOLS:** Keyhole saw, utility knife, fish tape, standard carpentry tools

Often the easiest way to fish cable is from a nearby receptacle. Before tapping into a receptacle, make sure you won't be overloading the circuit (see pages 134–135). Shut off the power. Remove the cover plate and see if the receptacle has a set of unused terminals. If it doesn't, add pigtails (see page 61) before reconnecting.

1 Open the box

Disconnect the receptacle. Check for a cable clamp or other device that will attach the new cable to the box. If necessary remove a knockout with a hammer and screwdriver and install a cable clamp.

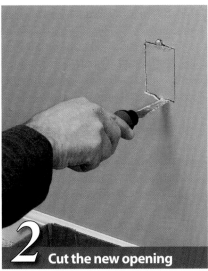

2 Cut the new opening

Use a box as a template to mark the new outlet opening. Cut the wall opening with a utility knife or keyhole saw. Locate the new box in the same wall cavity as the source box if possible.

CUT NOTCHES

Nail plate

To run cable past a stud, cut the wall covering across the stud. Save the cutout piece. Chisel a notch in the stud, lay in the cable, and install a nail plate to protect the cable. Patch the wall.

3 Connect fish tapes

Thread one fish tape (or bent coat hanger) through the knockout hole and another through the new opening. Wiggle one or both until they hook together. Pull the tape from the existing box through the new opening. Strip some sheathing from the cable, hook the wires to the end of the fish tape, and wrap with electrical tape.

4 Pull the cable through

Pull the cable through the new opening and into the old box. Connect the cable to the old box (see page 61), and install the new box (see page 64).

Running cable through the ceiling

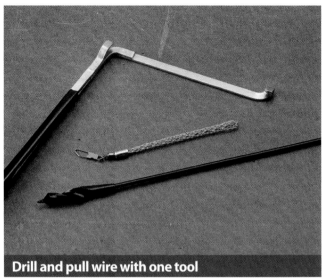

Run cable between joists

To minimize holes in the ceiling, run cable in the same direction as the joists whenever possible. Where you must run the cable across joists, use a stud finder to locate the joists and cut holes that are large enough to stick your arm through. Using a drill equipped with a long bit, bore holes through the joists and thread the cable through.

Drill and pull wire with one tool

A fishing bit allows you to run cable across joists or studs with a single tool. Drill through two joists or studs and leave the bit in place. Attach the cable to the end of the bit and pull it back through both holes.

Running cable into the basement

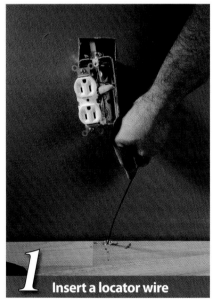

1 Insert a locator wire

To run wire down into a basement with an unfinished ceiling, pry off the base shoe or the baseboard. Drill a locator hole at the box location and thread a straight wire down through the hole.

2 Drill up through the wall

Go to the basement and find the locator wire. Drill a hole up through the center of the wall—about $2\frac{1}{4}$ inches from the wire for a 2×4 stud wall with $\frac{1}{2}$-inch drywall.

3 Run the cable

You may be able to have a helper poke the cable up through the hole in the basement and wiggle it; when you see it grab it. Otherwise insert a fish tape down through the hole in the wall and the hole in the floor, attach the cable, and pull it up.

Running cable behind baseboards and casing

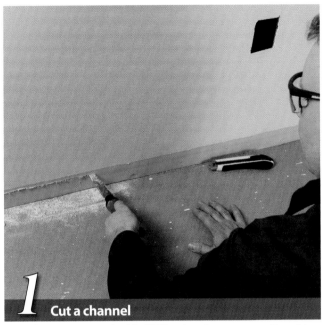

1 Cut a channel

For safety run armored cable (MC) rather than nonmetallic cable (NM) whenever you are snaking it behind a piece of molding. Remove a baseboard and cut away a strip of drywall or plaster low enough that the opening will be covered when you replace the baseboard.

2 Drill holes or cut notches

Drill holes through the centers of the exposed studs if there is room. If space is tight use a reciprocating saw or a handsaw to cut notches in the studs. You will likely encounter nails as you do so. Trim the nails back so they cannot damage the cable.

3 Run and protect the cable

Feed the cable through the hole where it will access power and through the holes or notches in the studs. Protect the cable by installing nailing plates at each stud.

4 Bring cable to the new outlet

If the hole for the new box is low enough, push the cable up through the wall to the hole. To pull the cable up to a higher opening, use a fish tape.

Run cable around doors

To run cable around a door, carefully remove the casing. Push the cable into the space between the jamb and the wall material, notching where necessary. If the jamb is tight against a stud, drill a hole in or notch the stud, thread the cable through the hole or notch, and run it up or down through the wall.

Patching walls and ceilings

- **TIME:** About 1 hour to install each patch and apply the first coat; applying the second and third coats takes about 15 minutes each
- **SKILLS:** Basic carpentry skills, smoothing joint compound, painting
- **TOOLS:** Utility knife, hammer, drywall saw, drill, taping knives of several widths, corner taping blade, drywall sander with sandpaper or screens

When running cable through finished rooms, try to minimize damage to walls. Neatly cut holes in drywall and keep the pieces you remove so you can replace them after the wiring is done. Plaster walls and ceilings are much more difficult to patch than drywall.

Before you start patching over your work, test the wiring thoroughly and have your building inspector review the work. If you cover the work before the inspection, you may be forced to tear out your patches.

A quality patching and painting job may take a full week. Usually at least three coats of joint compound will have to be applied, allowed to dry, and sanded smooth. Then the surface can be primed and painted to match the surrounding area.

1 Cut backer pieces to fit into the hole

Drywall patching kits make it easy to patch small holes, but for larger holes it's just as fast to install backerboards to support pieces of drywall. Cut the backer pieces from 1×4 lumber or strips of plywood about 6 inches longer than the width of the hole.

2 Attach the backers

Slip each backer piece into the hole, center it, and hold it while you drive 1¼-inch screws into it through the surrounding drywall. If you saved the drywall pieces when you made the cutout, they will fit perfectly. Otherwise cut new drywall to fit.

PATCHING MATERIALS

For strength use dry-mix joint compound for the first coat. (Do not use compound labeled "easy sand.") A bag labeled "90" will take about 90 minutes to harden; a bag labeled "45" will take 45 minutes to harden. You can apply additional coats of compound as soon as the first coat hardens, but you must wait longer for the compound to actually dry before you can paint. For additional coats apply ready-mix joint compound (it comes in a bucket), which is not strong but is easy to sand.

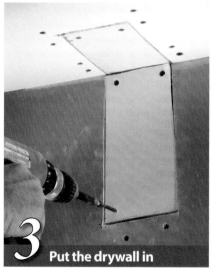

3 Put the drywall in

Scrape the patch edges free of loose paper and gypsum chunks. Attach the patches to the backers with screws. Sink the screw heads just below the surface of the paper face, but not deep enough to tear it. Cut pieces of fiberglass mesh tape to cover the joints; it's OK if an inch or so of a joint is not covered. Press the tape firmly onto the wall over the joints.

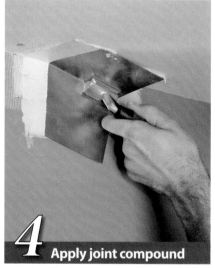

4 Apply joint compound

Mix a batch of joint compound so it is free of lumps and about the thickness of toothpaste. If your patch is at a corner, as shown, first use a drywall corner knife to apply compound. Concentrate on the inside corner; you will smooth the outer edges later.

5 Finish taping

Use a straight taping knife, at least 6 inches wide, to smooth the patch. Be patient; with practice you can become proficient. Feather the outer edges for a smooth transition to the wall. Allow the first coat to harden, then scrape away any protrusions.

6 Apply additional coats, then sand

Add a second coat, allow it to dry, then sand it smooth. To cut down on dust, you can use a damp sponge instead, although the result will be less smooth. Apply and sand succeeding coats until the surface feels smooth when you run your hand over it. Apply primer and paint.

Repairing plaster

1 Cut out and apply a drywall patch

Chip away all the loose plaster, including anything that feels spongy when you press on it, surrounding the hole. Measure the thickness of the plaster and buy drywall that is no thicker. Take your time to cut a patch that fits the hole fairly neatly. Drive a series of 1¼-inch drywall screws through the drywall and into the lath.

2 Tape the joints

Fill the joints with joint compound, then apply mesh tape over the joints. Apply a coat of joint compound over the tape and follow the steps shown above to scrape the first coat and apply and smooth succeeding coats.

Running cable in unfinished space

■ **TIME:** 1 hour to install two boxes and run 10 feet of cable
■ **SKILLS:** Drilling holes, fastening boxes in place
■ **TOOLS:** Drill with spade bit, hammer, lineman's pliers, saw, chisel

I f you're working on a new addition, or if you've gutted a room and removed the old walls, running cable will be much easier. Begin by installing the electrical boxes (pages 62–63). Place all the receptacles and switches at uniform height—12 to 16 inches from the floor for receptacles, 48 inches for switches. (See page 82 for more about box location.) Make sure the boxes protrude past the face of the studs so your drywall or other finish material will be flush with their front edges. Once the boxes are in place, follow these steps to run cable to the boxes.

1 Bore the holes to run cable

An electric drill and a ¾-inch spade bit can quickly bore holes for a run of cable. Keep extra bits on hand for large jobs—they will get dull. Align the holes by eye or use a chalkline to mark a guide. Bore as near the center of each stud as possible to maintain the strength of the framing and lessen the chance of drywall or trim nails piercing the cable. Drill straight through the studs for ease of feeding cable through the holes.

2 Run the cable

Run the cable fairly taut so it does not hang between studs. At corners you may need to bend the cable sharply to keep it at least 1¼ inches from the outer face of the framing. Leave a loop of 6 to 8 inches of cable at each box. This loop provides a margin of error if the wire is damaged when stripped and also makes future repairs and improvements easier.

3 Protect the cable

If a hole is less than 1¼ inches from the face of a framing member, attach a nail plate. Inexpensive and easy to install, it shields the wires from being pierced by nails or screws. Tap the nail plate into place with a hammer.

4 Drill or cut notches at corners

At an inside corner you can usually drill a hole in each direction. The two holes should intersect so you can thread the cable. Bend the cable and thread it through, pulling with a lineman's pliers.

If the corner is built up with several studs, it may be easier to cut notches for the cable with a handsaw or a reciprocating saw followed by a chisel. Be sure to cover the notches with nailing plates.

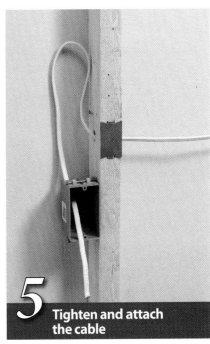

5 Tighten and attach the cable

Feed the cable into the box, leaving a 6- to 8-inch loop. Secure the cable in the box with a cable clamp. Most codes require stapling the cable to the framing member within 12 inches of the box, except cables fished through finished walls.

6 Drill plates for vertical runs

Drill holes in the top and bottom wall plates with a ¾-inch spade bit. Place the holes near the center of the plates. You may need to use a drill extension to bore through 2×4 plates. To avoid burning up the bit, stop periodically to let it cool. Drill at high speed and push gently.

7 Secure the vertical cable

On vertical runs secure the cable with insulated staples about every 4 feet, wherever you change direction, and 8 to 12 inches from each box. Avoid sharp bends in the cable.

Running cable in attics and floors

How you run cable in an attic depends on the attic's accessibility and usability. Some local codes allow cable to be surface-mounted in seldom-used spaces. Cable can be attached to the top of the joists with insulated staples. Nail 1×2 guard strips on either side to help protect the cable from damage.

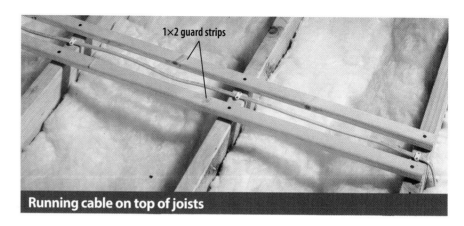

Running cable on top of joists

1×2 guard strips

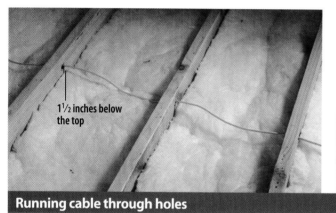

1½ inches below the top

Running cable through holes

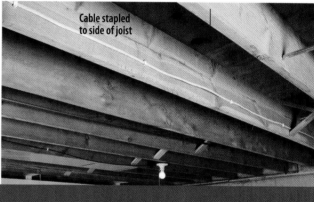

Cable stapled to side of joist

If your attic is readily accessible, bore holes through the joists, at least 1½ inches below the top of the joists (see photo, above). For the best protection—and to add a utilitarian floor—install plywood over the joists. If the attic has flooring, remove some of it to install the cable, or take an alternate route along framing members. In a basement run cable through holes in the joists.

SPECIAL PROTECTION

Special rules may apply when running cable in permanently unfinished space. Check the local codes before you do any work. Some codes require protection for cable in an attic when it is within 6 feet of the entrance, in a garage or basement when it is within 8 feet of the floor. Conduit is most commonly accepted for protection.

Strapping thicker cable

Because the heavy cable (8-gauge or larger) used for 240-volt appliance circuits is too stiff to thread easily through holes in joists, some codes allow wiring to be strapped to the underside of joists and along joist plates. Check your local code—conduit may be required for all exposed runs.

Connecting cable to boxes

Cable should be firmly connected to a box or to a nearby framing member. Consult local codes to find the method that your building department recommends. This page shows the most common methods for connecting nonmetallic cable to boxes. Other connectors are needed for armored cable, Greenfield, and conduit (see pages 77 and 80).

In most cases, it is easier to strip the sheathing—but not the wire insulation—before you run the cable into the box. It's easy to damage the wire insulation if you strip sheathing from the cable in a box.

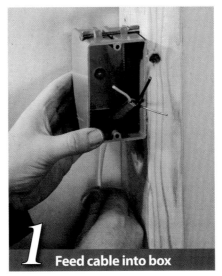

1 Feed cable into box

Some plastic boxes have capture holes with spring fingers that grab the cable as you push it through. The capture hole keeps the cable from sliding back out of the box but does not clamp the cable firmly. Metal boxes have different types of clamps, shown below.

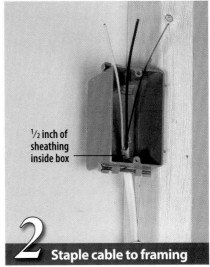

½ inch of sheathing inside box

2 Staple cable to framing

Secure the cable to the framing with an approved cable staple. Codes usually require a staple within 12 inches of the box, except where cables have been fished through finished walls. Some codes require a cable loop between the staple and the box so you can pull more cable into the box in case of wire damage.

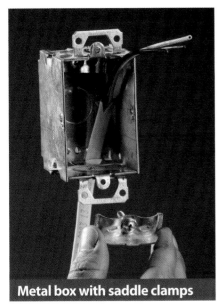

Metal box with saddle clamps

Some metal boxes come with internal saddle clamps. Tightening the saddle clamp's screw firmly secures one or two cables. Pull only one cable through each hole.

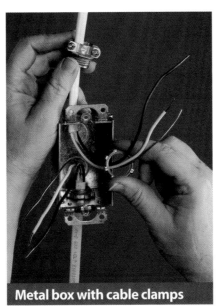

Metal box with cable clamps

Cable clamps vary depending on the type and size of cable you are running. Remove a knockout hole in the box, then attach the clamp to the box by tightening the locknut. Run the cable through the clamp and tighten the two clamp screws to secure the cable. Or you can attach the clamp to the cable first, run the cable into the box, and tighten the locknut.

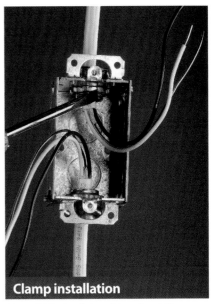

Clamp installation

About ½ inch of sheathing should be visible in the box so the clamp can grip the sheathing, not the wires. Twist the locknut on using your fingers, then push a straight screwdriver against the ears on the nut to tighten it.

Working with armored cable

Flexible armored cable, or BX, is composed of a bendable metal sheathing containing insulated and ground wires. Greenfield, or flexible conduit, is a hollow flexible metal sheath. Like conduit it is a tube that holds wires. Check local codes regarding the use of these materials since restrictions vary. (See page 48 for the different types of wire and cable available.)

CAUTION

SHARP EDGES CAN DAMAGE WIRE

The cut ends of these metallic sheathings are sharp. If wires rub against the ends, insulation could be stripped, resulting in an electrical short. Follow these procedures carefully to protect the wires at all times.

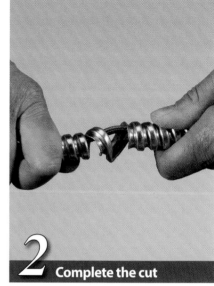

1 Nick and bend the cable

Hold a hacksaw at a right angle to the spirals and just barely nick the sheathing. Do not cut into the wire insulation inside. Bend the cable over and squeeze until it folds (see inset above).

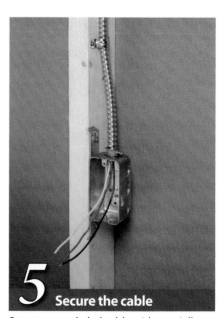

2 Complete the cut

Twist the armor and it will snap free. The paper-wrapped wires (and aluminum bonding strip, if there is one) can be snipped with ordinary wire cutters. To expose the wires for connections to boxes and fixtures, cut off the armor at a second point about a foot away from the end.

3 Thread through holes in framing

Run armored cable and flexible conduit through holes bored in the middle of framing members. It can run through notches where necessary. These materials are heavier and stiffer than nonmetallic cable, so it will take more room to make turns.

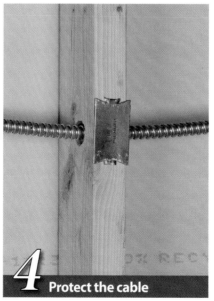

4 Protect the cable

Even armored sheathing can be pierced with a nail, so anywhere that the cable is within 1¼ inches of the framing surface, protect it with a nail plate. Check your local codes to see if short runs of flexible armored cable can be left exposed.

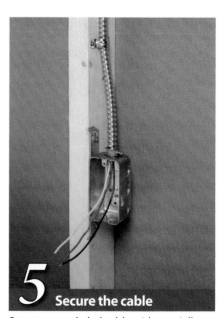

5 Secure the cable

Support metal-clad cable with specially designed straps or staples approximately every 4 feet and within 12 inches of boxes. If you're fishing through existing walls or ceilings, secure the run as best you can.

Connecting armored cable

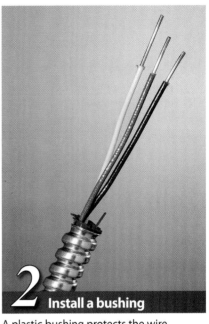

1 Choose the connectors

In most cases use a straight connector that holds the cable in place either by clamping it or with a setscrew. You may need to use a 90-degree or 45-degree connector in some situations. To install a connector, choose the side of the box you wish to access and remove a knockout. Cut the cable to length and trim off the armored sheathing (see opposite page).

2 Install a bushing

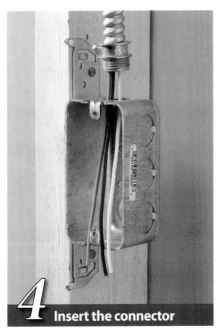

A plastic bushing protects the wire insulation from abrasion. Pull the brown paper surrounding the wires back about an inch inside the armor. This leaves room to slip in a bushing. If your cable has a bonding strip, fold it back.

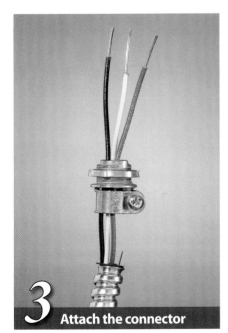

3 Attach the connector

Slip on a connector, making sure the bushing is in place. Tighten the clamp or setscrew to secure the cable.

4 Insert the connector

Slide the wires and connector into a knockout hole, slip on a locknut, and tighten with your fingers. As with all wiring connections should be made only in boxes.

5 Tighten the locknut

Tighten the locknut with a hammer and screwdriver. Tug on the cable to make sure everything is securely fastened.

Cutting and assembling conduit

■ **TIME:** About 2 hours for a run with three bends and two boxes
■ **SKILLS:** Careful measuring, clean cutting, screwing pieces together
■ **TOOLS:** Hacksaw, pliers, screwdriver, conduit reamer

Codes sometimes require conduit, especially where exposed wiring would be susceptible to damage. Conduit has definite advantages: It protects the wires, and the electrical system can be upgraded later by pulling new wires through the conduit. Conduit is the most difficult way to install wiring because it's hard to bend. But it is still within reach for do-it-yourselfers. For small jobs use elbows and connectors at each turn to avoid bending conduit.

Codes allow conductors to fill only a certain percentage of the cross section of the conduit (see page 49), though it often might seem possible to squeeze in more wires. In many cases it's better to install larger conduit than your project might need—say, ³/₄-inch instead of ¹/₂-inch—to allow for added circuits in the future.

1 Measure and cut

Measure the distance for the run—don't forget to subtract for the connector or elbow you will be using. Cut conduit with a hacksaw or a tubing cutter. Hold conduit against a cleat or use a miter box to keep it from rolling as you saw.

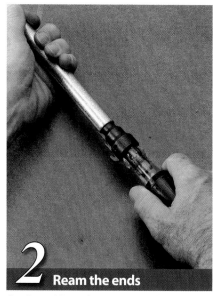

2 Ream the ends

Cutting with a tubing cutter or hacksaw leaves burrs inside the end of the conduit that can chew up wiring insulation in a hurry. Remove them from the inside of the conduit using a conduit reamer. Smooth rough spots on the outside as well so the conduit can slip easily into a connector.

3 Install a junction box

Where you have more than four turns to negotiate, install a junction box. When it's time to pull the wires, it will let you start another run. More boxes and few bends ease wire-pulling.

Offset connector

Use an offset connector to keep the conduit close to the wall when it's attached to a box. The conduit can be bent to form an offset (see opposite page), but adding an offset connector is easier.

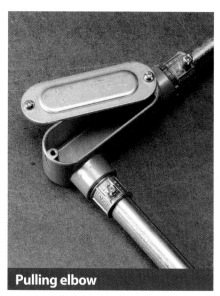

Pulling elbow

A pulling elbow makes negotiating corners easier. Remove the cover to pull the wires through. Don't make any connections inside a pulling elbow; wires must pass through without a break.

Bending conduit

■ **TIME:** About 30 minutes to measure, bend a piece, and connect it on either end
■ **SKILLS:** This is a specialized skill that requires practice
■ **TOOLS:** Conduit bender, tape measure, black marking pen

For larger jobs it is expensive and time-consuming to use connectors at each corner. Instead bend the conduit. Bending isn't difficult, although getting the bend in just the right location is tricky and requires some practice.

Runs begin and end at places where you can get at wires to pull them. Codes generally forbid a total of more than 360 degrees of bends in a run. Before you start bending add up the degrees of the bends you'll be making in a single run to ensure the total is less than 360 degrees.

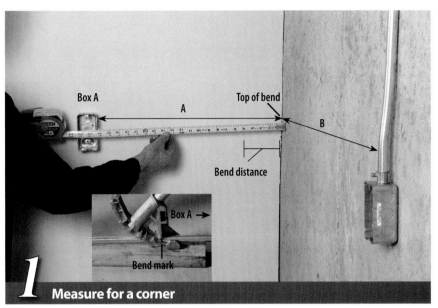

1 Measure for a corner

To bend conduit around a corner, first measure from the box to the top of the bend (distance A). Then subtract the bend distance from that and make the bend mark on the conduit that distance from the end. (The bend distance for ½-inch conduit is 5 inches. For ¾- and 1-inch conduit, allow 6 and 8 inches, respectively.) Slip the conduit bender onto the tubing and align the index mark on the bender with the bend mark, as shown in the inset photo.

2 Form a smooth curve

Pull slowly and steadily on the handle. For extra force, you can step on the back of the bender. Tugging too sharply will crimp the tubing, and you'll have to start over with another piece. (Codes forbid installing crimped conduit, which could chafe wire insulation.) Making crimp-free bends takes practice. After making the bend, trim section B by holding the bent conduit in place for measuring. Cut the end so it reaches the box.

Offsets: Start with a 15-degree bend...

When mounting conduit on a flat surface, you'll need to form an offset at each box. Offsets must be aligned with other bends in the tubing. A stripe painted along the length of the conduit helps you do this. First make a 15-degree bend.

Then bend it the other way

Roll the conduit over and move the bender a few inches farther from the end. Then pull until the section beyond the first bend is parallel to the floor.

Connecting and anchoring conduit

One-hole strap on masonry wall

Barbed strap driven into wood

Two-hole strap on wood

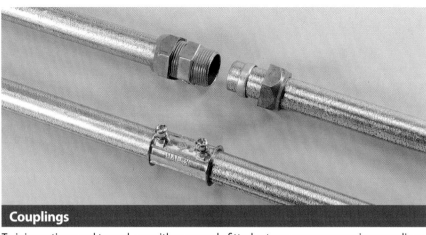

Couplings

To join sections end to end, use either securely fitted setscrew or compression couplings.

Compression connector

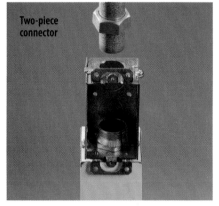

Two-piece connector

Setscrew connector

Angled compression connector

Anchoring the conduit

Anchor conduit runs with at least one strap every 8 feet and within 3 feet of every box. Attach straps with screws or nails. For masonry walls use screws and plastic anchors. On framing drive barbed straps into the wood.

To mount conduit inside walls, bore holes in the studs or notch the framing and secure conduit with straps or metal plates every 8 feet.

Box connectors

Box connectors differ mainly in the way they attach to conduit. Compression connectors grab the conduit as you tighten the nut with a wrench. To install a setscrew connector, slip it on and tighten the screw.

All these connectors attach to the box with the same threaded stud and locknut arrangement used with cable connectors (see page 75). Insert the stud into a knockout hole, turn the locknut finger tight, then tap the nut with a hammer and screwdriver to tighten it. A two-piece connector comes in handy when space is tight inside a box. Instead of a locknut it has a compression fitting. As you tighten the nut, the fitting squeezes the conduit.

Pulling wire through conduit

- **TIME:** A few minutes to 1 hour to pull wires through a conduit run
- **SKILLS:** Basic electrical skills
- **TOOLS:** Fish tape, lineman's pliers

When you start pulling wire through conduit, you start to realize why codes are so specific about bends, crimps, and burrs in conduit. Pulling wire can be surprisingly hard work. If you suspect that the wire is scraping against something that might damage the insulation, stop work, locate the trouble spot (you can find it easily by using the wire as a measuring device), and remove it. Apply pulling lubricant to the wires if you need to make a long pull.

1 Push through short runs

For short runs with only a couple of bends, you can probably push the wires from one box to the other. Feed the wires carefully to protect the insulation.

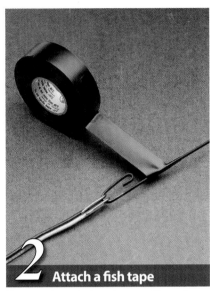

2 Attach a fish tape

If you can't push the wires, you'll need a fish tape and an assistant. Snake the fish tape through the conduit, hook the wires to the fish tape and secure with electrician's tape. Wrap the connection neatly so it can slide through the conduit.

3 Pull the wires through

As one worker feeds the wire in and makes sure there are no kinks, the other pulls. Pull the wires with steady pressure—avoid tugging. As the wires work past bends, expect to employ more muscle. If you have lots of wires or a long pull, lubricate the wires with pulling grease. Where possible use gravity to aid the process. Feed wires from above and pull from below.

4 Leave plenty of wire in the box

Leave 6 to 8 inches of wire at each box. Never splice wire inside conduit—all wires must run continuously from box to box.

Outlet locations

The general rule for locating outlets in a room is simple: No point horizontally along the floor line of the walls of a room can be more than 6 feet from an outlet. Any wall space longer than 2 feet is included, but doors, fireplaces, and similar openings or breaks do not count as wall space. Windows do count. The intent is to prevent running cords across door openings and the like and to minimize the need for long extension cords. On a long, straight wall, outlets could be as far as 12 feet apart. It is better to install more outlets than necessary in a room than too few. Always check local codes for specific requirements.

Consider installing floor outlets in rooms where tables or conversational furniture groupings will be placed away from walls. If a floor outlet is more 18 inches from a wall, it does not count as a wall outlet as far as the 6-foot rule is concerned. Outlets for specific appliances, such as a washing machine, must be 6 feet or less from the appliance. Place multiple outlets, ideally on separate circuits, in locations where a number of devices will be plugged in—the wall where an entertainment center will be placed, for instance, or in a home office.

No point on a kitchen countertop can be more than 24 inches from an outlet, and a separate outlet should be provided for the refrigerator. An island or peninsula larger than 12×24 inches must have enough receptacles to meet the 24-inch distance. Where there is no backsplash or wall, outlets can an be installed 12 inches or less below the rim of a contertop, but outlets may not be installed faceup. Always check local codes for specific requirements..

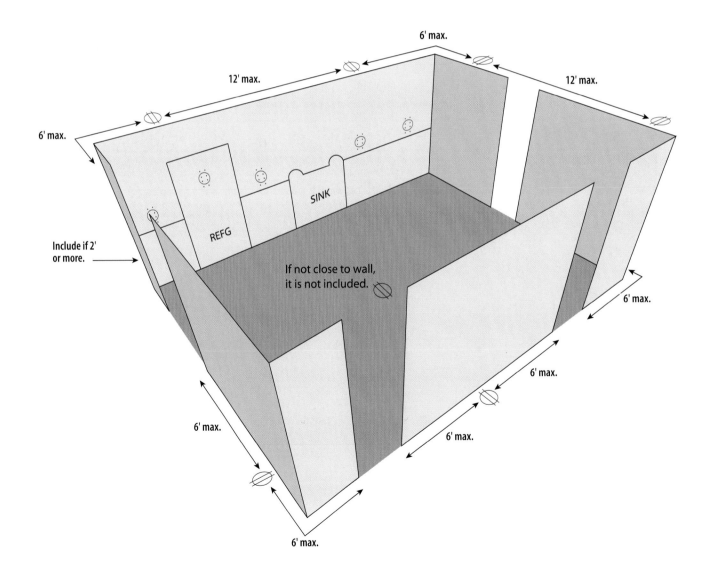

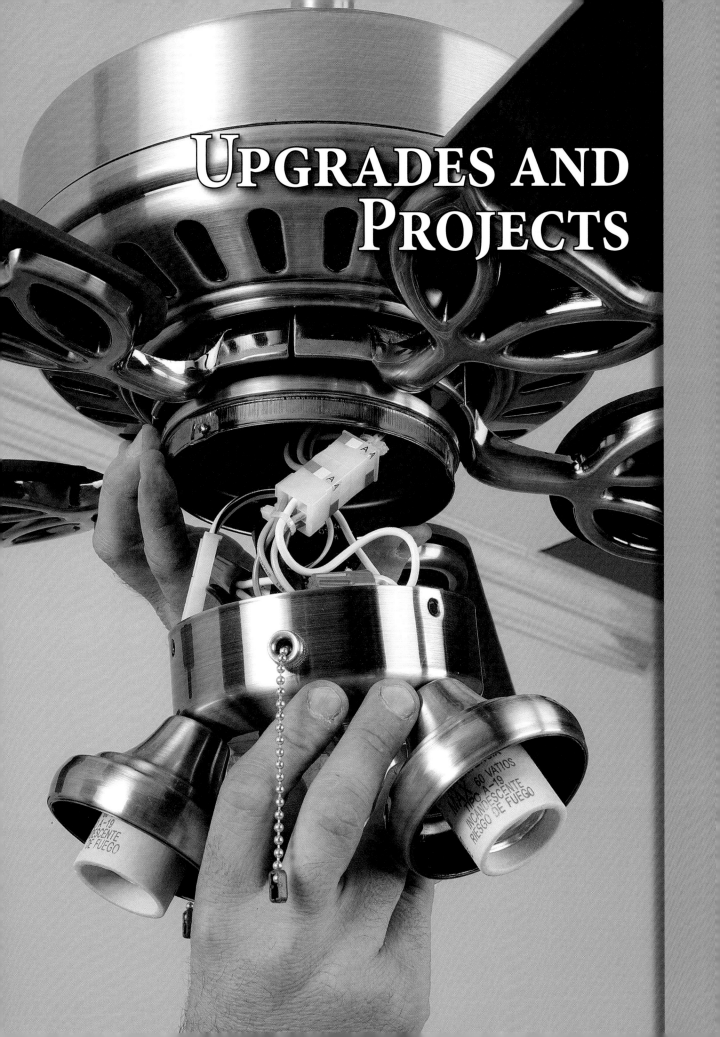

UPGRADES AND PROJECTS

Installing special switches

- **TIME:** About an hour to install most of the switches on these two pages
- **SKILLS:** Connecting wires
- **TOOLS:** Screwdriver, lineman's pliers, wire stripper

One of the easiest ways to upgrade your home's electrical system is to install special switches. Wiring them is usually about as simple as installing a standard switch.

There are many options, so choose the switch that best meets your needs. The least expensive dimmers have round switches that you twist. Sleeker options include the sliding dimmer, right, or dimmers that look like regular toggle switches. Other types allow you to choose a level of brightness and then turn the light on and off at that level. Motion-sensor switches turn on a light fixture whenever someone enters a room and stay on for a prescribed amount of time.

Some switches have limitations. An ordinary dimmer, for example, can only dim incandescent bulbs and may be limited to a total of 600 watts. For higher-wattage fixtures, such as a chandelier with many bulbs, buy special dimmers able to handle 800, 1,000, or 1,500 watts. (For more information on these and other switches, see pages 50–51.)

If you have ground wires, they all should be connected together in the box, no matter what kind of switch you are installing.

Always shut off the power before removing or installing a switch.

Single-pole dimmer

Most dimmers have wire leads instead of screw terminals. Hook up a single-pole dimmer as shown.

Most dimmers are larger than conventional switches, so you may have to rearrange wires in the box before you can fit one in. Don't force a dimmer in because the case might crack. If there are too many wires, order a thin-profile unit.

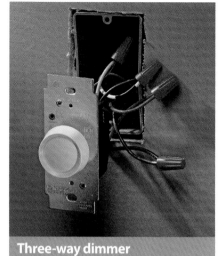

Three-way dimmer

Three-way dimmers have three hot leads. Before you remove the old switch, determine which is the common terminal—it will be identified on the switch body or the screw will be darker-colored than the others. Hook the common wire to the new switch's common lead and connect the other wires to the remaining leads. (For more on three-way switches, see pages 104–106.)

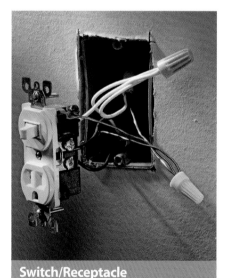

Switch/Receptacle

In this wiring arrangement the receptacle is always hot and not controlled by the switch. Connect the ground wires (see page 61). Attach a white pigtail to the silver terminal and splice it to the other white wires. Connect the feed wire to a terminal that has a connecting tab. Join the other black wire to the brass terminal that does not have a connecting tab.

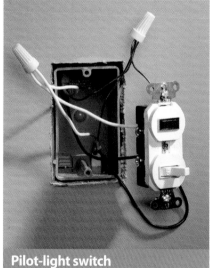

Pilot-light switch

This switch has a bulb that glows when its fixture is on. Attach the black feed wire to the brass terminal on the side that does not have a connecting tab. Pigtail two white wires and attach them to the silver terminal. Connect the black wire that leads to the fixture to the terminal on the side with the connecting tab.

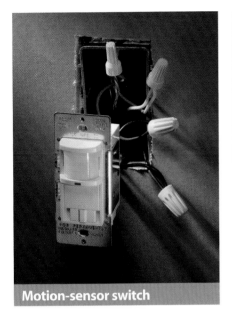

Motion-sensor switch

An infrared beam detects movement and turns on a light fixture. A time-delay feature lets you choose how long the light remains on. Connect the neutral wires to each other, not to the switch. Attach the black feed wire to one lead and connect the black wire that runs to the fixture to the other lead.

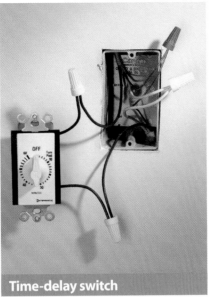

Time-delay switch

You can program this switch to turn off a fixture with a delay ranging from 1 to 60 minutes. In addition to the clock timer switch shown, electronic switches with presettable delays are available. Connect the black leads to the black wires in the box and join the white wires together, not to the switch.

Fluorescent dimmer

Fluorescent dimmer switches install the same way as incandescent dimmers (see opposite page), but you must equip each lamp with a special ballast. Remove the fixture. Mark the wires with tape so you'll know where to refasten them. Remove the lamp holders and disconnect their wires by poking a nail or thin screwdriver into the terminals. Take off the old ballast and install a new dimming ballast. Reconnect the lamp holders. Reinstall the fluorescent fixture. If more than one fluorescent light is connected to a dimmer switch, all the bulbs must be the same size and share the same ballast. (For replacing a ballast, see page 29.)

Double switch

This unit has two switches that fit into a single-switch space. Attach the feed wire to a terminal on the side with the connecting tab. (This tab enables the wire to supply power to both switches.) Connect the two wires that lead to the two fixtures to the terminals on the other side and join the white wires together, not to the switch.

Plug-in lamp dimmer

A lamp dimmer is a simple way to provide variable-level lighting. To install it just plug the dimmer cord into a receptacle and plug a lamp into the back of the dimmer plug. Turn the lamp switch on and control the lamp with the dimmer switch. You can place the dimmer near the lamp or in any convenient location you can reach with the cord.

MONEY SAVER

These switches give you greater control over your lighting and can save money as well: A dimmer switch enables you to operate a bulb at less than its full intensity so you save energy and prolong the life of the bulb. Time-delay and pilot-light switches are energy-efficient solutions too. You can also buy programmable switches to save money and provide security while you are on vacation. You can program them to turn lights on and off in a pattern that makes it appear you are still at home.

GFCI devices

Fuses and circuit breakers protect the wiring in your home. A ground fault circuit interrupter (GFCI) protects people from getting a dangerous shock.

A GFCI has a microprocessor that senses tiny current leaks and shuts off the power instantly. In most circumstances a leak isn't a big problem. In properly grounded systems most stray current is carried back to the service panel. What remains would scarcely give you a tickle. But if you are well grounded—standing on a wet lawn or touching a metal plumbing component, for example—that tiny bit of current would pass through your body on its way to the earth. As little as $1/5$ of an amp, just enough to light a 25-watt bulb, can be dangerous.

A GFCI connects to both wires of a circuit so it can continuously compare current levels flowing through the hot and neutral sides. These should always be equal. If the microprocessor senses a difference of just $1/200$ of an amp, it trips the circuit to interrupt power in $1/40$ of a second or less, cutting off the electricity before you're seriously hurt. Any ground fault is a potential hazard. If a tool or appliance is faulty, it can give you a serious shock even if its grounding wire is in good condition. So GFCI protection is a good idea anywhere you might be in contact with water while using electricity, such as in a kitchen, in a bathroom, or outdoors.

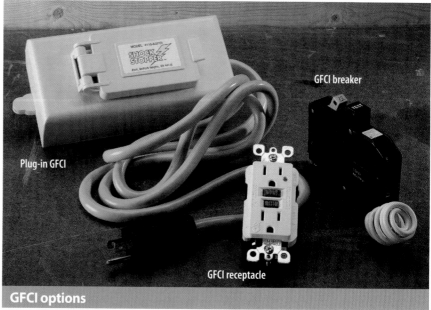

GFCI options

There are three types of GFCIs: plug-ins, receptacles, and breakers. To install a portable plug-in unit, simply insert its blades into a receptacle and plug in the appliance. A GFCI receptacle replaces a conventional receptacle, and properly placed can protect other receptacles on the same circuit. Install a GFCI breaker into a service panel to protect a circuit.

GFCIs are required in some places

Electrical codes require GFCI receptacles in places where you're likely to ground an electrical appliance. In a kitchen codes often require GFCIs for all receptacles within 6 feet of a sink. All bathroom receptacles, as well as all outdoor receptacles, must be GFCI-protected.

Installing GFCI devices

TIME: About 1 hour
SKILLS: Connecting wires
TOOLS: Screwdriver, lineman's pliers, wire stripper

1 Connect hot and neutral wires

You can clip a GFCI breaker into a service panel as you would an ordinary breaker (see page 137), but you must wire it differently. Shut off the main breaker and be careful not to touch the hot wires coming into the box. Select the circuit you wish to protect, unclip the old breaker from the hot bus bar, and slip it out of the service panel. Disconnect the hot wire from the old breaker and the neutral wire from the bus bar. Attach both wires to the setscrew terminals of the new GFCI breaker. Strip ½ inch of insulation from the pigtail.

2 Ground and install the breaker

Loosen a terminal on the neutral bus bar and connect the white pigtail from the breaker by inserting the wire and tightening the screw. Clipping the GFCI breaker into place attaches it to the hot bus bar. Turn the power back on, set the breaker, and push the test button. The breaker should trip.

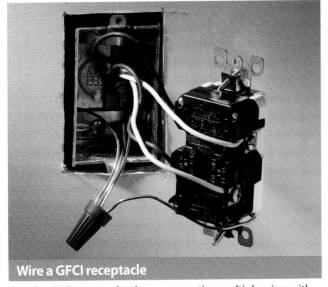

Wire a GFCI receptacle

Attach a GFCI receptacle, above, connecting multiple wires with pigtails. Incoming power goes to the LINE terminals. LOAD lines carry power from the GFCI to other receptacles on the circuit. If you install a GFCI as the first receptacle of a circuit, the rest of that circuit will also be protected. If you are installing a GFCI at the end of a line, cap the load leads with wire connectors or buy a version that protects only one receptacle.

MAKE MORE ROOM FOR A GFCI

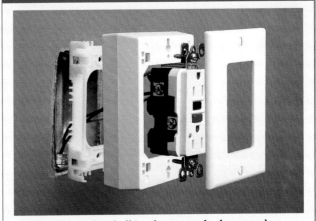

A GFCI receptacle is bulkier than a standard receptacle, so it may be a tight fit in a box. If gently pushing the wires back doesn't help the GFCI fit, then don't force it. You might break the case or loosen the wire connections. Instead install a box extender.

Adding surge protection

■ **TIME:** About 15 minutes
■ **SKILLS:** Joining wires
■ **TOOLS:** Screwdriver, wire stripper, lineman's pliers

O ccasionally your electrical service can experience sudden sharp increases in power, known as surges. A surge usually will not harm lights and appliances, but it could damage sensitive electronic equipment, such as a computer.

To protect a few pieces of equipment, buy a surge protector that plugs into an outlet. Or replace an existing receptacle with a surge-protecting receptacle.

Install one the same way you would a normal receptacle. Follow the manufacturer's instructions for connecting the wires on the device to the wires in the wall box.

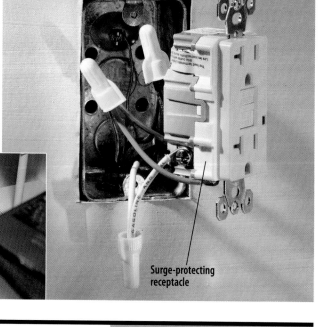

Plug-in unit

Surge-protecting receptacle

Adding surge arresters to circuits

■ **TIME:** About 1 hour
■ **SKILLS:** Understanding of your service panel
■ **TOOLS:** Screwdriver, tongue-and-groove pliers, wire stripper

T o protect a circuit against surges, install a surge arrester in your service panel. At the service panel shut off the main circuit breaker and take off the panel cover. Remove the ½-inch knockout nearest to the circuit you want to protect. Insert the surge arrester through the knockout hole and fix it in place by tightening the nut. Cut the wires as short as possible for maximum protection. Attach the white wire to the neutral bus bar and the black wires to the breakers for the circuits you want to protect.

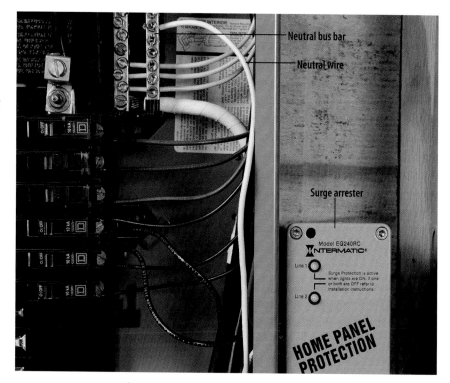

Neutral bus bar

Neutral wire

Surge arrester

Model EG240RC
INTERMATIC

Line 1

Surge Protection is active when lights are ON. If one or both are OFF refer to installation instructions.

Line 2

HOME PANEL PROTECTION

Installing wall sconces

- **TIME:** About a full day to install a new switch and two sconces, not including any wall patching
- **SKILLS:** Basic electrical skills, cutting and patching walls
- **TOOLS:** Keyhole saw, screwdriver, lineman's pliers, drill, fish tape

Wall sconces are ideal for hallways, stairways, and any room that needs indirect accent lighting. Installing a wall sconce is similar to adding a new light fixture. The only difference is the location and type of fixture box used. As with ceiling lights you can control as many lights as you want with one switch. You can control one or more lights from two different locations by using three-way switches. See pages 103–107 for the various options.

Ideally you want to secure the fixture box to a framing member as well as the drywall or plaster. Use one of the standard retrofit boxes (see page 55).

LIGHTING WITH WALL SCONCES

Wall sconces provide a splash of indirect light, creating the illusion that a room is larger than it is. For this reason, and because they are commonly placed slightly higher than eye level, keep the bulb wattage low.

In most cases wall sconces work best in conjunction with other lights rather than as the primary light source for a room. They work well for ambient light but are insufficient for specific tasks, such as reading.

Install sconces 72 to 78 inches high. Any lower and you will bump into them; any higher and they will seem designed to light the ceiling rather than the room.

Typically it makes the most sense to add wall sconces to one wall requiring accent or indirect lighting. A few sconces go a long way, so keep them spaced more than 6 feet from each other.

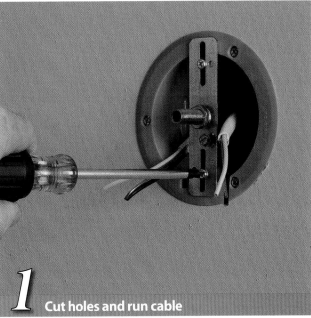

1 **Cut holes and run cable**

Shut off the power. Find a junction box or a receptacle with power you can use. Cut a vertical hole for the switch box and horizontal or round holes for the sconce boxes (see page 64). Run cable from the power source to the switch and from the switch to the holes (see pages 66–69). Fasten cable to the boxes, allowing an extra 8 inches of cable to protrude at each box. Attach the boxes to the walls.

2 **Connect the wires**

Strip the sheathing and the wire insulation, then make the electrical connections (see pages 58–61). Note that wires travel both into and out of the first sconce fixture box. Wire the switch (see page 102).

3 **Install the sconce**

Tuck the wires into the box, screw a mounting strap to the box, and attach the sconce to the mounting strap. Secure the switch and its cover plate and test.

Installing ceiling fixtures

■ **TIME:** 1 hour to mount a simple fixture; more time is needed for elaborate units
■ **SKILLS:** Basic carpentry and wiring skills
■ **TOOLS:** Screwdriver, pliers

Dramatically change the appearance of a room by adding or replacing a ceiling light. Although there are many choices, from plain ceiling fixtures to elaborate chandeliers, all install in essentially the same way: Power comes through a ceiling-mounted box that is designed to support the fixture. If you are replacing a ceiling fixture, take the time to inspect the wires and the area around the outlet box for heat damage (see page 19).

1 Remove the old fixture

Shut off the power. Remove the globe or diffuser and the bulbs. Then remove the screws or the cap nut holding the canopy in place and drop the fixture down. Disconnect the black and white wires. Check the wires for cracks in the insulation and replace if needed (page 27).

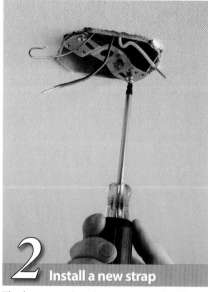

2 Install a new strap

The box may already be equipped with mounting hardware compatible with your new fixture. If not install a new strap. Some ceiling fixtures come with a strap and may have other mounting hardware.

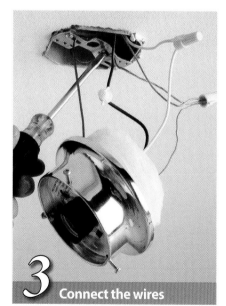

3 Connect the wires

Support the fixture with a bent coat hanger so both hands are free to do the wiring. Connect the ground wire either to the box's ground wire or to the box itself (see page 61). Splice the fixture's white lead to the box's white wire and the black lead to the black or colored wire and twist on wire connectors (see pages 58–60).

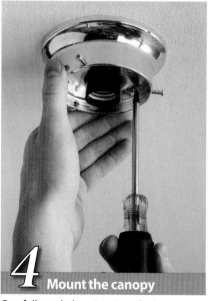

4 Mount the canopy

Carefully tuck the wires into the box and push the canopy into position. If the canopy mounts with two screws, start each of them into the holes in the strap. Check again that the wires are all tucked away and tighten the screws. If the fixture mounts with a center nut, see the instructions on the opposite page.

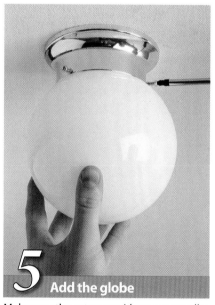

5 Add the globe

Make sure the setscrews (there are usually three) are just started into the threaded holes in the side of the canopy; they should not protrude in yet. Push the globe into the canopy's lip, check that it is all the way up, and gently tighten the setscrews.

Installing a pendent light

1 Install a nipple

Shut off the power. Remove the old fixture (see opposite page). Install a strap that has a threaded center hole, if necessary. Screw a nipple (a short length of threaded tubing) into the strap so it hangs down far enough to mount the pendent light's canopy.

2 Connect the wires

If the light has a chain, remove links as needed so the light will hang at the desired height. Check to see if the canopy will fit (next step). Thread wires up through the chain and cut them to length so they will fit comfortably in the box. Connect the ground wire. Splice the neutral (ribbed) wire to the box's white wire and the hot wire to the box's black or colored wire.

3 Attach the canopy

Restore the power and test the light with a circuit tester. Turn the power off again. Carefully tuck the wires into the box, slide the canopy up, and tighten the mounting nut onto the nipple.

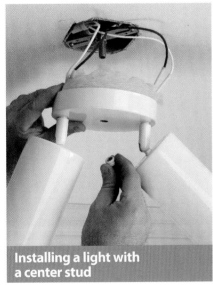

Installing a light with a center stud

If a fixture's canopy has a single hole in the middle, it mounts using a fixture stud or a nipple. The stud or nipple pokes through the canopy just far enough to attach the nut. Cut the stud rather than screwing it deep into the box, which could damage the wiring. Splice and tuck the wires into the box, slide the canopy over the stud, and screw on the mounting nut.

Ceiling light with swivel strap

If you need to rotate the fixture for best appearance, install a swivel strap. Wire the fixture and mount it as you would a standard fixture but hold off the final tightening until you are certain of the fixture's alignment.

Medallions

If your ceiling is damaged around the ceiling box, a fixture with a wide canopy may cover up the imperfections. To cover a larger area, or for a decorative touch, install a medallion. Most come with double-sided tape to hold them in place while you install the light.

Installing track lighting

■ **TIME:** 4 to 6 hours for a 12-foot system if you are working from an existing ceiling box

■ **SKILLS:** Connecting wires in a box, attaching to a ceiling

■ **TOOLS:** Tape measure, phillips screwdriver, drill with screwdriver bit

Track lighting offers a lot of flexibility. After it is installed you can easily change the type and number of lights, their positions, or the direction they aim.

The initial hookup is similar to other ceiling fixtures (see page 90). Installing the tracks, though, so they are properly aligned in your room, involves measuring your ceiling and establishing lines for correct placement. Have two ladders and one helper on hand for placement. (If you do not have an existing box to connect into, see pages 64–65.)

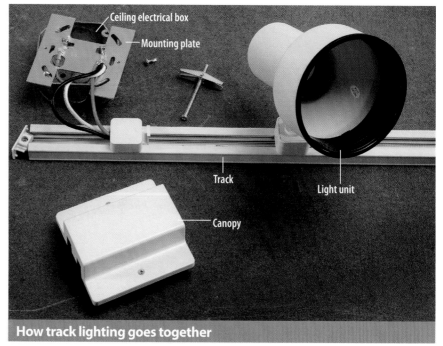

How track lighting goes together

Instructions for your lighting equipment will tell you specifically how to make connections. Most track lights go together in the following way: A mounting plate connects to the ceiling electrical box and transfers power to metal contact strips inside the track; a canopy covers the connections. Each light unit has two contacts at the base. These conduct power to the light from the electrified contact strips in the track. Most units pivot so they can highlight a specific area.

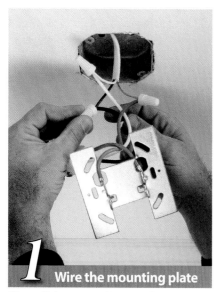

1 Wire the mounting plate

Shut off the power. Remove the existing light. Connect the plate's ground wire (see page 61). Following the manufacturer's instructions connect the mounting-plate leads or terminals to the box wires—white to white and black to black or colored (see pages 58–60).

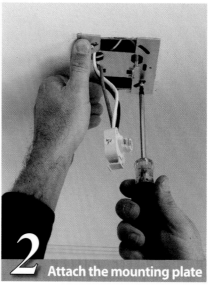

2 Attach the mounting plate

Tuck the wires carefully into the box, push the mounting plate into position, and drive screws into the box's strap. Locate joists with a stud finder and determine how you will attach the track (step 5).

3 Add the track

Cut the track or tracks to the desired length using a hacksaw. While a helper holds the other end, position the track on the mounting plate and attach it.

4. Measure for track alignment

While your helper continues to hold the track, measure out from the wall and position the track parallel to the wall.

5. Attach the track to the ceiling

If the track runs across joists, drive mounting screws through the track and into the joists. If the track runs parallel to the joists, drill holes approximately every foot, tap in plastic anchors, and drive screws into the anchors.

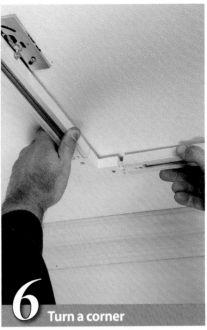

6. Turn a corner

When your setup includes an angle, snap a 90-degree elbow onto the end of the track you just installed. While a helper holds the other end, slide the new track onto the elbow. Attach the new track as you did the first. Cover all open ends.

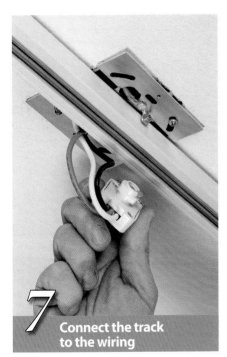

7. Connect the track to the wiring

The mounting plate has a connector that makes an electrical connection with the track. Push the connector into the track and twist it so it seats firmly. Snap the canopy over the connector.

8. Install the lights

Some track lights are screwed onto the track using a metal arm. Others, as shown, simply twist on. Position the lights where desired, restore power, and test. Move the lights or rotate them to achieve the illumination you desire.

TRACK LIGHTING OPTIONS

You can run track lighting in just about any configuration. In addition to the L fitting shown in step 6, you can buy a flexible fitting that can make a turn of any angle, a T fitting, or a cross-shape fitting.

Track lights (lamps) are available in a variety of styles. You can install several types of lights on the same track to suit different purposes—for instance, you could have several floodlights illuminating walls with one spotlight shining on a work of art or a cabinet full of glassware.

Installing Eurostyle lights

- **TIME:** 2 to 3 hours once you've decided on the layout
- **SKILLS:** Connecting wires in a box, measuring, installing hardware
- **TOOLS:** Tape measure, lineman's pliers, wire stripper, drill with screwdriver bit, screwdriver

This is an inexpensive way to add a decorative touch. Similar to track lighting this system allows you to move and reorient the individual lights.

The basic installation is straightforward. However expect to spend some time planning the route of the track. You may want to hold the track up against the ceiling in various configurations to determine which arrangement works best.

Several styles are available. Some feature a track that can be bent into curves, others have rigid tandem poles, and others have twin wires. In each case individual lights hang from the tracks or wires.

A transformer located in the canopy reduces power to about 12 volts, so the electrical parts are not dangerous once installed and turned on. However the basic connection uses standard household current, so be sure to shut off the power before installation.

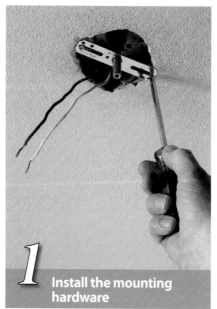

1 Install the mounting hardware

Shut off the power. Remove the existing ceiling fixture or run power to a new ceiling box (see pages 101–102). Install the strap and the stud (short threaded rod) that comes with the light.

2 Wire the mounting plate

In this model three fixture leads connect to the house wires, and three others connect to the canopy. Thread the wires for the canopy through the hole so they protrude downward. Connect the other ground wire (see page 61). Splice the white lead to the box's white wire and the black lead to the black or colored wire (see pages 58–60).

3 Attach the mounting plate

Tuck the wires into the box and thread the mounting plate over the stud and up against the box. Add the washer and nut and tighten the nut.

4 Connect the wires and attach the canopy

Connect the leads to the terminals on the canopy. Push the canopy up onto the mounting plate and twist it to lock it in place. Add side screws to hold it firm.

5 Lay out and attach the anchors

Determine the path you want the track to follow on your ceiling and make pencil marks indicating the anchor locations. Keep the anchors evenly spaced. At each location drill a hole, tap in a plastic drywall anchor, and attach the light anchor by driving a screw.

6 Attach the track

Insert a rod into each anchor and tighten a setscrew to hold it firm. Working with a helper push the track into all the rods. Screw on a cap at each rod but do not tighten. Reexamine the layout, adjust the track if needed, then tighten the caps.

7 Install the lights

Slip each light's base up onto the track and screw on the cap. When the lights are arranged as you like, tighten the caps.

Another type of light

Some Euro lights dangle from two wires. Keep a light like this out of the reach of small children to avoid accidents. The wires are actually hot when the light is turned on, although they are not dangerous because they carry only low voltage. A canopy containing a transformer hooks to the ceiling fixture and connects to the wires via wires of the same type.

Installing recessed lights

- **TIME:** About 3 hours to install four lights, after running the cable from the switch
- **SKILLS:** Cutting a clean hole in the ceiling, running cable through joists, attaching wires
- **TOOLS:** Drill with screwdriver bit, drywall saw, keyhole saw, fish tape, fishing drill bit, wire stripper, lineman's pliers, screwdriver

Recessed fixtures are a good choice if you need plenty of light but don't want it to stand out visually. Because each fixture has its own integral electrical box, there is no need to install electrical boxes, making this the easiest way to add new (as opposed to replacement) lighting.

If you are installing multiple recessed lights, plan the layout on a piece of graph paper. Whenever you run into a joist you will have to move the light over several inches.

CAUTION

PREVENT HEAT PROBLEMS

A recessed light builds up a lot of heat, which can lead to ceiling damage, melted wire insulation, and possibly fire. Keep building insulation at least 3 inches away from fixtures; if ceiling insulation will come within 3 inches of a recessed light you must install a fixture rated insulated compatible (IC). Don't place fixtures in a cramped space. Use bulbs of the recommended type and wattage. Remove flammable materials, such as scraps of insulation paper, near the fixture.

1 Mark the ceiling for a hole

Mark the centers of all the planned lights. Use a stud finder or drill a small hole and insert a bent wire to check for nearby joists. Adjust the hole positions if needed. Place the fixture's cardboard template on the ceiling and trace the cutline.

2 Cut a hole

Cut the holes in the ceiling with a drywall saw. If the ceiling is plaster, cutting will be more difficult. Start with a knife, then switch to a keyhole saw, taking care not to vibrate the lath, which can cause the plaster to crack.

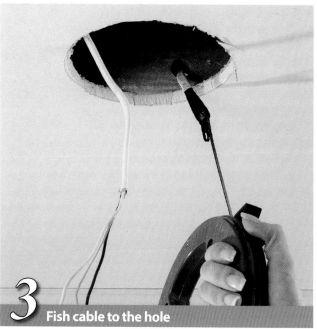

3 Fish cable to the hole

For tips on fishing cable, see pages 66–69. If you are running cable perpendicular to the joists, drill a hole in a nearby joist. Then cut access holes and drill holes in the other joists that you must cross. Using a fishing bit on a drill can eliminate the need for some access holes.

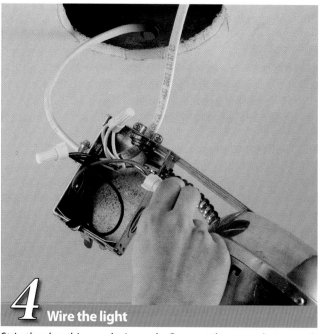

4 Wire the light

Strip the sheathing and wire ends. Connect the ground wires and splice the white lead to the white wire(s) and the black lead to the black or colored wire(s). Tuck the wires into the fixture's junction box and close the cover.

5 Thread the can into the hole

Position the can's mounting clips so they will not get in the way. Carefully insert the cables and the junction box up into the hole. Then push the can up so its lip is against the ceiling.

6 Anchor the fixture

The fixture grasps the ceiling drywall or plaster via three clips. Use a screwdriver to push up on the clip, which causes the part outside the box to move downward. Each clip should click into place.

7 Install a light trim

Various trim options are available. The type shown connects via two pairs of spring hooks. Squeeze one pair, insert the ends into the can's holes, and let go. Repeat with the other pair. Push the trim up until it snaps into place. Other trims connect via coiled springs, which also attach to holes inside the can.

Installing a new-work fixture

If the joists are exposed, install a light designed for new construction. Slide the mounting bars outward and fasten each to the joist with a nail or screw. Then slide the can to adjust its position.

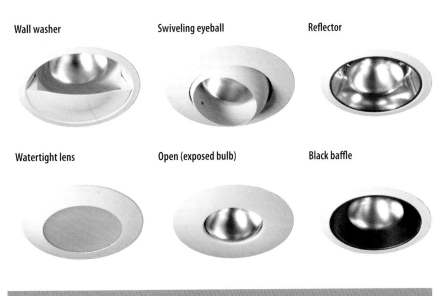

Wall washer   Swiveling eyeball   Reflector

Watertight lens   Open (exposed bulb)   Black baffle

Trim options

An eyeball trim can be swiveled to point at a feature on the wall or a tabletop. A reflector trim increases the brightness of the light. Use a wall washer trim to highlight a section of the wall. If you are installing lights in a damp location, use a trim with a watertight lens.

Installing undercabinet fluorescent lights

■ **TIME:** Plan 1 day to run cable and install 6 or 7 lights

■ **SKILLS:** Running cable, stripping and connecting wires, cutting and patching walls

■ **TOOLS:** Stud finder, drywall saw, drill, fish tape, lineman's pliers, wire stripper, screwdriver

Lighting positioned on the underside of kitchen wall cabinets provides bright illumination, but does not shine in the eyes of an adult standing at the counter.

You may choose to install low-voltage halogens (see page 100), but they get very hot. If you have only one or two lights to install, consider purchasing undercabinet fluorescent fixtures that plug into a nearby receptacle. If you want to add a section of lights controlled by one or two switches, you may choose to run cable and install a series of fluorescents.

Select fixtures that are 1½ inches thick. One-inch-thick fixtures are sleeker but more difficult to install because there is little room for cramming in wires.

This job is much easier to do while the wall cabinets are removed, so it is an ideal project when replacing wall cabinets. Mark the walls with lines that show precisely where the new cabinets will be installed and run the wiring so that the cabinets will cover most (if not all) of the holes in the wall.

Local codes for undercabinet lights vary; strict codes may require you to run conduit or armored cable, and you may be required to install an electrical box behind every fixture.

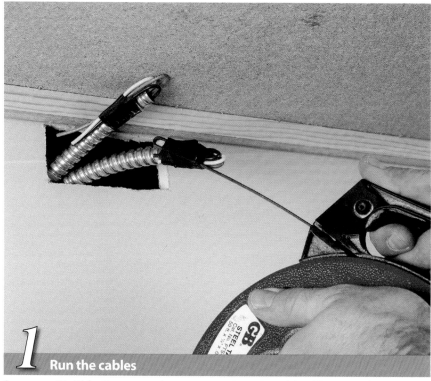

1 Run the cables

See pages 66–68 for tips on running cable. This is much easier to do if the wall cabinets are not yet installed.

If you can, remove the countertop's backsplash and cut a channel that will later be covered when you replace the backsplash. Before you cut holes for the lights, check each light to determine where the cable will enter and exit. You may be able to cut holes small enough so they will be covered by the lights.

Drill holes in the studs and install protective nailing plates. Run cable from a power source to the switch box. Then run cable from the switch box to the lights. Allow plenty of cable at each connection.

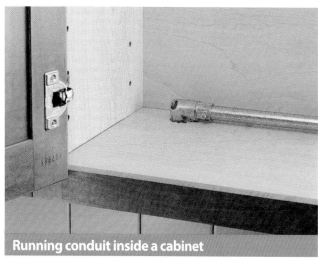

Running conduit inside a cabinet

Rather than cutting holes in the wall, local codes may allow you to run conduit or armored cable inside the cabinets. Use elbow connections to direct the wires down into the light fixtures.

Adding raceway under a cabinet

Raceway wiring is another option for wiring the lights. This will save cutting and patching the wall and saves space inside the cabinets. See pages 110–111 for installation tips.

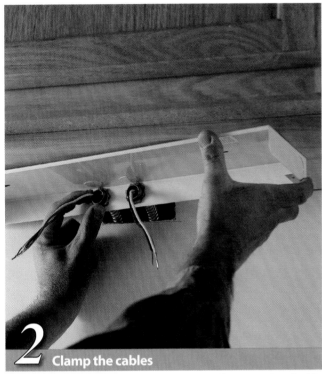

2 Clamp the cables

Strip enough sheathing so the wires can reach connections inside the light. Disassemble each light. Clamp the cables to the light's housing as shown.

3 Attach the housing

Guide the cables into the wall as you push the housing against the wall and the underside of the cabinet. Drive screws to secure the housing.

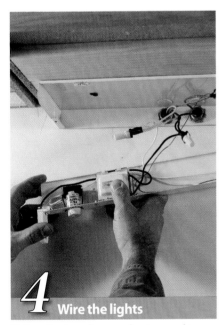

4 Wire the lights

Determine how long each wire needs to be; plan splices in places where there is ample room for the wire connectors. Connect the ground wires (see pages 60–61). Splice the white leads to the white wires and the black leads to the black wires. Snap the light together and add fluorescent tubes.

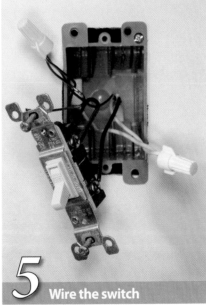

5 Wire the switch

Shut off the power. Install a remodel box and run the cables through it. Attach the cable at the power source. Connect the ground wires (see pages 60–61). Splice the two white wires together and connect the two black wires to the switch. Restore power and test the lights. Snap on the light covers.

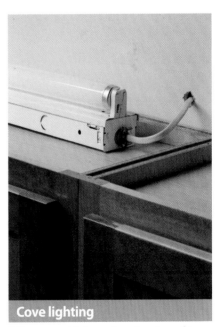

Cove lighting

A fluorescent fixture placed on top of a wall cabinet throws dramatic illumination upward and outward. Because the fixture is not visible, you can buy an inexpensive unit and let the wiring hang out.

Adding undercabinet halogen lights

- ▓ **TIME:** About a day to install a switch and 10 lights
- ▓ **SKILLS:** Stripping and connecting wires, simple carpentry skills
- ▓ **TOOLS:** Screwdriver, drill, lineman's pliers, keyhole saw

A kitchen is a brighter, more pleasant place to work when its countertops are illuminated by undercabinet fixtures. Undercabinet lighting provides a sparkling decorative effect and excellent task lighting.

A 120-volt system requires hours of fishing cable and installing fixture boxes in one of the most crowded and complicated areas of the house. An attractive alternative is the low-voltage system shown here. Low-voltage halogen lights operated with a remote-controlled, surface-mounted switch can be installed in a day and look as good as a more permanent system. Power for multiple lights is supplied by a single transformer mounted inside the cabinet. Because the transformer simply plugs into a standard 120-volt receptacle, new cable or boxes are usually not needed.

1 Locate fixture and install transformer

Determine a location for each light fixture where it won't shine in your eyes as you work. Keep in mind halogen lights can be safely attached to wooden cabinets but get hot and should be kept away from plastic and paper goods. Remove the trim ring and lens from each fixture base and attach them with screws to the underside of the cabinets. (Be sure the screws are the right length so they do not poke up into your cabinet.) Align the fixtures so the bulbs face the same direction. Drill holes to allow the wires to pass into your cabinet and plug their ends into the transformer located inside the cabinet. Coil excess wire inside the cabinet. Drill a hole and run the power cord from the transformer to a 120-volt receptacle.

LOW-VOLTAGE LIGHTING TRANSFORMERS

Halogen lights suitable for undercabinet installation often come with a transformer that plugs into a receptacle. A cord from the lights plugs into the unit. The one shown above powers two lights; more lights would require a larger one. You can install a receptacle inside a cabinet to hide the transformer.

2 Assemble the lights

Once the fixture bases are installed, snap the lens cover onto the reflector ring. Some undercabinet lighting kits come with a warning label to attach inside the cabinet door, cautioning users about the heat of the units.

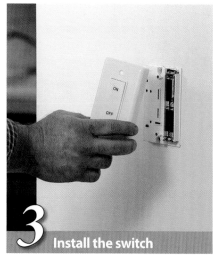

3 Install the switch

The remote-control switch operates by battery power, so it can be installed anywhere in the kitchen and requires no wiring. Attach the switch housing by screwing it to the wall—use plastic anchors if you can't find a stud. Screw the cover plate to the switch housing.

Wiring a ceiling fixture

■ **TIME:** About 1 hour making connections, not including running the cable and installing boxes
■ **SKILLS:** Basic electrical skills
■ **TOOLS:** Lineman's pliers, needle-nose pliers, side-cutting pliers, wire stripper, cable ripper, screwdriver

Depending on which way is easier to run cable, you can wire a ceiling fixture with the power coming into the box (as shown on this page) or with power coming into the switch (as shown on page 102).

Here, as with the configurations on pages 102–107, the type of fixture doesn't matter. Whether it is a flush-mounted light, track lighting, a chandelier, or a ceiling fan, the rough wiring to the fixture is the same.

Power source

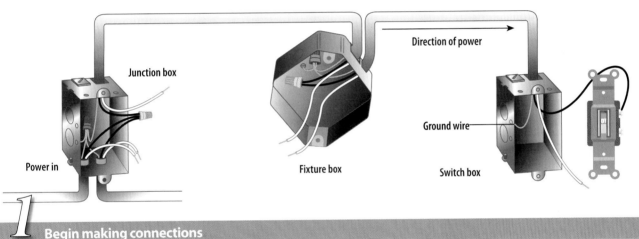

Junction box

Direction of power

Ground wire

Power in

Fixture box

Switch box

1 Begin making connections

Shut off the power. Install the fixture box and a switch box and run cable as needed (see pages 66–68). Find a junction box or receptacle box that has power from a circuit you can use. Run two-wire cable from the junction box to the fixture box and from the fixture box to the switch. Connect the ground wires (see pages 60–61). Attach all the black wires as shown. Note how the black wire picks up power at the junction box and carries it to the fixture box, then on to the switch.

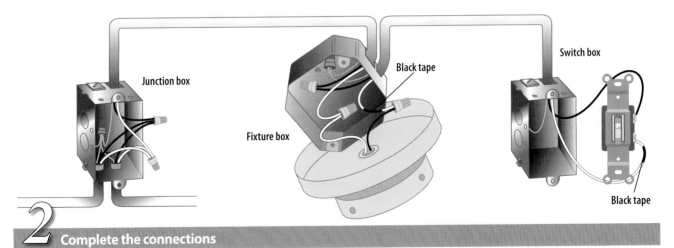

Junction box

Black tape

Switch box

Fixture box

Black tape

2 Complete the connections

Mark the white wire running from the switch box to the fixture box with black tape on both ends. Attach one end to the switch. At the fixture box connect the black-taped white wire to the black fixture wire and the untaped white wire to the white fixture wire. At the junction box connect all white wires together. (For instructions to connect the wires, see pages 60–61.)

Wiring two ceiling fixtures

■ **TIME:** About 1½ hours to plan and complete the connections, not including running the cable and installing boxes
■ **SKILLS:** Basic electrical skills
■ **TOOLS:** Lineman's pliers, needle-nose pliers, side-cutting pliers, wire stripper, cable ripper, screwdriver

In this wiring configuration power comes to the switch first, then goes to both of the fixtures. (A single light also can be wired this way.) A single switch can control many fixtures. Just extend the run from one to the next. If you have multiple fixtures on a single line, make sure the wattage or amperage total of the fixtures doesn't exceed the maximum indicated on the switch.

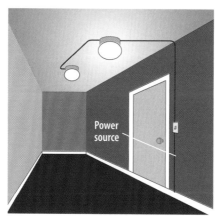

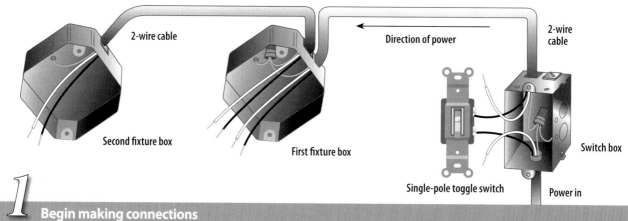

1 Begin making connections

Shut off the power. Install the fixture boxes and a switch box and run cable as needed (see pages 66–68). Find a junction box or receptacle box that has power from a circuit you can use. Run two-wire cable from the junction box to the switch box. Then run the cable from the switch box to the first fixture box, and from

that box to the next fixture box. Connect the ground wires (see pages 60–61). At the switch box hook both black wires to the terminals. The current in the black wire passes through the switch to the first fixture box.

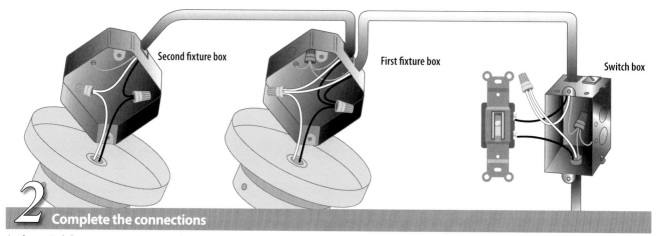

2 Complete the connections

At the switch box connect the two white wires together. At the first fixture box, join all three black wires together and connect all three white wires together. At the second fixture box, attach the black wires together and connect the white wires together. Note that you also can control two or more fixtures with the power

coming to the fixture, but it's more complicated. Route the power as on page 101 and attach the second fixture's black wire to the black-taped white wire in the first fixture box. (For instructions to connect the wires, see pages 60–61.)

Wiring separate switches

- **TIME:** About 1½ hours to make connections, not including running the cable and installing boxes
- **SKILLS:** Basic electrical skills
- **TOOLS:** Lineman's pliers, needle-nose pliers, side-cutting pliers, wire stripper, cable ripper, screwdriver

I f you are installing ceiling fixtures and a switch box, with a little more work you can provide individual switches for the fixtures. Use a two-gang box for the switches or a double switch in a single box and run three-wire cable between the fixtures and to the switch. Power comes to the fixtures through two-wire cable. Electricians like three-wire cable because in many instances it allows the use of one cable instead of two.

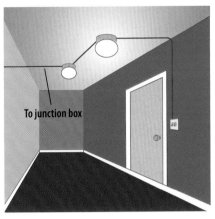

To junction box

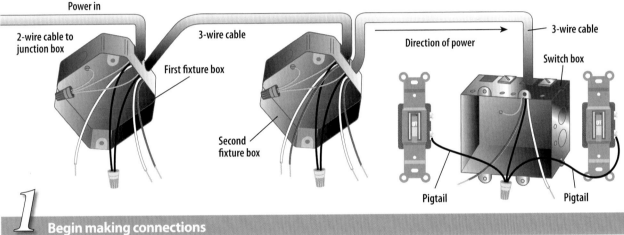

Power in

2-wire cable to junction box

3-wire cable

Direction of power

3-wire cable

First fixture box

Second fixture box

Switch box

Pigtail

Pigtail

1 Begin making connections

Shut off the power. Install the fixture boxes and a switch box and run cable as needed (see pages 66–68). Run two-wire cable from a junction box to the first fixture box. Run three-wire cable from the first to the second fixture box and from there to the switch box. Connect all ground wires (see pages 60–61). Bring power to the switches by attaching the black wires in all three boxes as shown. In the switch box cut pigtails (short pieces of wire) and connect them to the switches.

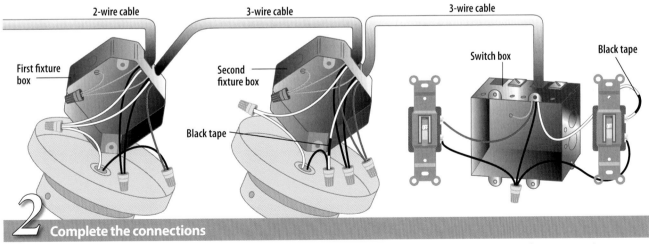

2-wire cable

3-wire cable

3-wire cable

Black tape

First fixture box

Second fixture box

Switch box

Black tape

2 Complete the connections

At the switch box connect the red wire to a switch and the white wire to the other switch. Wrap black tape on the white wire, both at the switch box and at the fixture box to show that it is hot. At the second fixture box, join the two red wires together. At both fixture boxes connect the hot and neutral wires to the fixture wires as shown. Or install this wiring configuration with power coming to the switch. Split the incoming black wire and run the outgoing red and black wires to the fixtures. The neutral white wire, shared by both switches, passes on through.

Wiring three-way switches

■ **TIME:** About 1½ hours to make connections, not including running the cable and installing boxes
■ **SKILLS:** Basic electrical skills
■ **TOOLS:** Lineman's pliers, needle-nose pliers, side-cutting pliers, wire stripper, cable ripper, screwdriver

Three-way switches control power to a fixture from two separate points, allowing you to control a ceiling light from either side of a room. Three-way switches use a three-wire system that has a power wire and two interconnecting wires called travelers. Unless you have metal conduit or armored cable, you also need a fourth, grounding wire. Power comes in through one switch, then travels to the fixture and to the second switch.

Power source

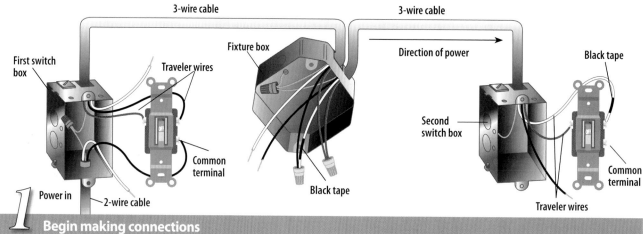

1 Begin making connections

Shut off the power. Install the switch boxes and a fixture box and run cable as needed (see pages 66–68). Run two-wire cable from a junction box or a receptacle box to the first switch box. Run three-wire cable from the first switch box to the fixture box, and from the fixture box to the second switch box. Connect all ground wires (see pages 60–61). At the first switch box, connect the hot wire to the common terminal on the switch (it is either labeled or darker than the other two). Attach traveler wires to the other two terminals. At the second switch box, attach the red and white wires to the noncommon terminals of the switch. Wrap a piece of black tape on the white wire, both here and at the fixture box. At the fixture box connect the two red wires and join the marked white wire to the black wire that comes from the first switch.

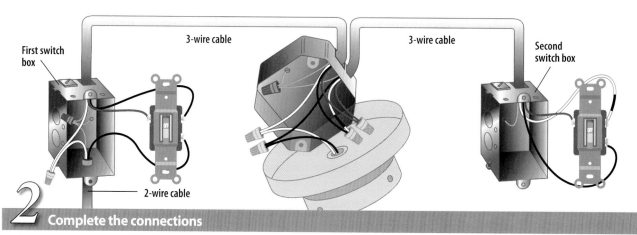

2 Complete the connections

At the second switch box, connect the black wire to the common terminal on the switch. This completes the hot portion of the circuit. At the first switch box, attach the two white wires. At the fixture box connect the white and black wires to the fixture. Once completed either switch will operate the light.

Wiring three-ways, power to switch

- **TIME:** About 1½ hours to make the connections, not including running the cable and installing boxes
- **SKILLS:** Basic electrical skills
- **TOOLS:** Lineman's pliers, needle-nose pliers, side-cutting pliers, wire stripper, cable ripper, screwdriver

Page 104 shows how to wire three-way switches when the light is between two switches. This page shows the light located beyond both switches and includes an example with a three-way dimmer. (Only one of the two switches can be a dimmer.)

For this configuration run three-wire cable between the switches. Power comes into the first switch and out of the second on just two wires.

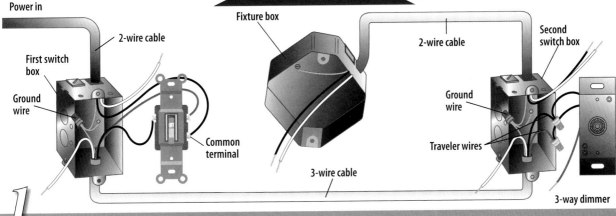

1 Begin making connections

Shut off the power. Install the switch boxes and a fixture box and run cable as needed (see pages 66–68). Run two-wire cable from a junction box or a receptacle box to the first switch box. Run three-wire cable from the first switch box to the second, and two-wire cable from the second switch box to the fixture box. Connect the ground wires (see pages 60–61). At the first switch box, attach the black (hot) wire of the power source to the switch's common terminal. Connect traveler wires to the other terminals. At the second switch box, connect the travelers. (Note: A three-way dimmer can burn out if hooked up incorrectly. Check it by setting up the circuit with ordinary three-way switches and turning on the power. Then replace one switch with a dimmer.)

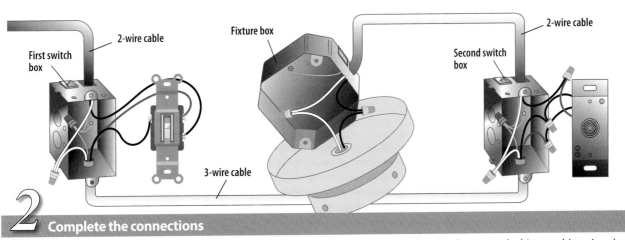

2 Complete the connections

At the second switch box, connect the black wire that goes to the fixture box with the dimmer's common wire. Join the two white wires. At the first switch box, attach the white wires. At the fixture box connect black to black wires and white to white wires. Install the switches, switchplates, and the light fixture.

Wiring three-ways, power to fixture

■ **TIME:** 1½ hours after running cable and installing boxes
■ **SKILLS:** Basic electrical skills
■ **TOOLS:** Lineman's pliers, needle-nose pliers, side-cutting pliers, wire stripper, cable ripper, screwdriver

In this situation power comes to the light fixture, then proceeds to the two switches. A two-wire cable runs to the fixture and to the the first switch box. A three-wire cable runs only from switch box to switch box.

ABC'S OF THREE-WAYS

Follow these principles when wiring three-way switches:

A. Always attach the incoming hot (black) wire to the common terminal of the first switch.

B. Use traveler wires to connect the traveler terminals on the switches to each other, never to the light.

C. Connect the common terminal of the second switch to the black wire from the fixture.

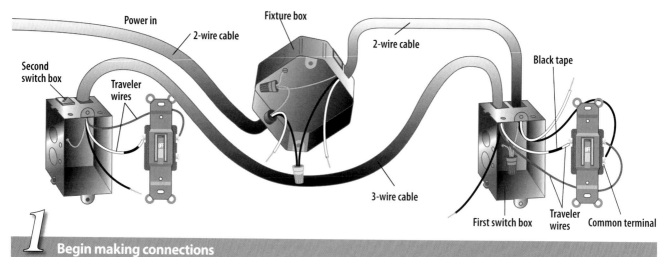

1 Begin making connections

Shut off the power. At the fixture box connect the black hot wires. At the first switch box, connect the hot wire to the common terminal and the traveler wires to the other terminals. Wrap a piece of black tape on either end of the white wire to show that it is hot. At the second switch box, attach the traveler wires.

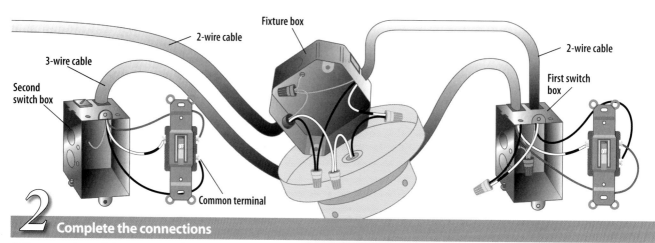

2 Complete the connections

At the second switch box, connect the switch's common wire to the black wire leading to the fixture box. Attach the two white wires. At the first switch box, connect the white wires. At the fixture box connect black to black wires and white to white wires. Install the switches, switchplates, and the light fixture.

Wiring four-way switches

- **TIME:** About 2 hours to make the connections for a fixture and three switches, not including running the cable and installing boxes
- **SKILLS:** Basic electrical skills
- **TOOLS:** Lineman's pliers, needle-nose pliers, side-cutting pliers, wire stripper, cable ripper, screwdriver

To control a fixture from three or more different switches, use one or more four-way switches. You can install any number of them between a pair of three-way switches. In four-way situations the first and last switches must always be three-ways.

Here, incoming power flows from switch to switch to switch then to the fixture, but it also could take one of the routes previously illustrated.

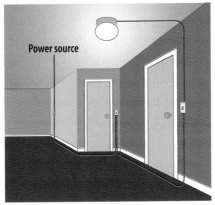

Power source

1 Begin making connections

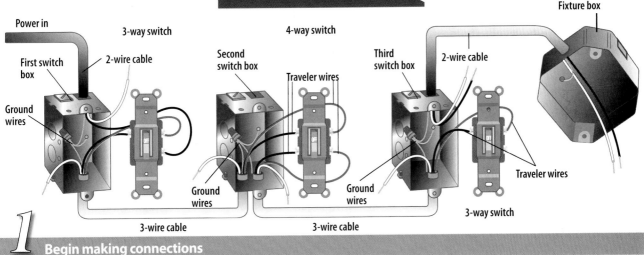

Power in · First switch box · 3-way switch · 2-wire cable · Ground wires · Second switch box · 4-way switch · Traveler wires · Third switch box · 2-wire cable · Fixture box · Traveler wires · Ground wires · Ground wires · 3-way switch · 3-wire cable · 3-wire cable

Shut off the power. Install the switch boxes and a fixture box and run cable as needed (see pages 66–68). Run two-wire cable from a junction box or a receptacle box to the first switch box. Run three-wire cable from the first switch box to the second and third, and two-wire cable from the third switch box to the fixture box.

Connect all ground wires. At the first switch box, attach the black wire from the power source to the switch's common terminal. Connect the traveler wires to the other terminals. At the second and third switches, connect the traveler wires as shown. The four-way switch carries only traveler wires.

2 Complete the connections

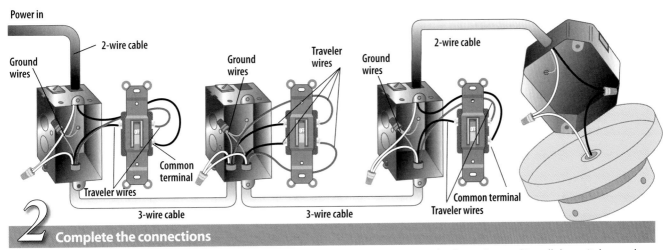

Power in · 2-wire cable · Ground wires · Ground wires · Traveler wires · Ground wires · 2-wire cable · Common terminal · Traveler wires · 3-wire cable · 3-wire cable · Common terminal · Traveler wires

At the third switch connect the fixture box's black wire to the common terminal. Join the white wires together. Attach the white wires at the first and second switch boxes. Connect the fixture to the two wires at the fixture box and install the switches and switchplates. Once completed you can turn the fixture on and off from any of the three switches.

Adding a receptacle

- **TIME:** About 1 hour to make connections, not including running the cable and installing boxes
- **SKILLS:** Basic electrical skills
- **TOOLS:** Lineman's pliers, needle-nose pliers, side-cutting pliers, wire stripper, cable ripper, screwdriver

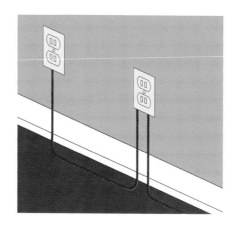

O nce you find a usable power source, adding a receptacle is easy to figure out. Most of the work involves cutting the wall, installing a box, fishing the cable, and patching the wall.

These instructions show how to tap into a receptacle at the end of the run. If the receptacle is in the middle of the run, it will have wires running to all of its terminals. Use wire connectors to connect a new line; see page 60.

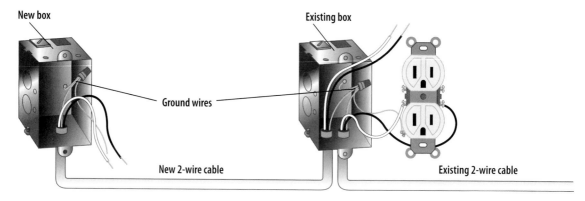

New box

Existing box

Ground wires

New 2-wire cable

Existing 2-wire cable

1 Begin making connections

Shut off the power. Find a receptacle box where you can draw power without overcrowding the box or overloading the circuit. (You also can draw power from a junction box. Just connect the hot and neutral wires to the receptacle.) Install the new receptacle

box. Run a two-wire cable from the existing box to the new box. Remove the screws that secure the existing receptacle to the box and pull it out so you can work on it. Connect the ground wires in both boxes as shown.

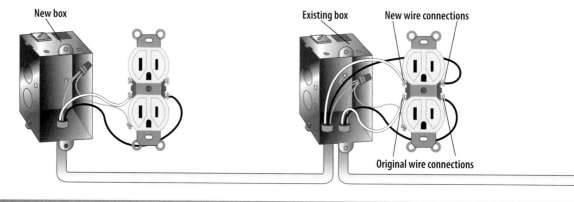

New box

Existing box   New wire connections

Original wire connections

2 Complete the connections

At the existing box connect the black wire to the hot receptacle terminal, which is brass-colored. Attach the white wire to the other terminal. At the new box also connect the black wire to the hot terminal and the white wire to the other terminal. Wrap both

receptacles with electrician's tape so all the terminals are covered. Fasten both receptacles in place, turn on the power, and test your installation. Attach the receptacle cover plates.

Splitting, switching receptacles

■ **TIME:** About 1 hour to make the connections, with the cables and boxes in place
■ **SKILLS:** Basic electrical skills
■ **TOOLS:** Screwdriver, wire stripper, lineman's pliers, needle-nose pliers

Examine a standard duplex receptacle and you'll see that each set of terminals on either side connects to a small metal tab—one silver-colored, one brass-colored. If you break this bridge, the upper and lower receptacles can be used independently, one controlled by a switch and one functioning like a standard receptacle. A split receptacle is handy when you want to turn a living room lamp on and off from a wall switch, for example, but still want to leave half of the receptacle for general use. Sometimes you may need a split receptacle when you want to supply the two outlets of a heavily used receptacle with two different circuits.

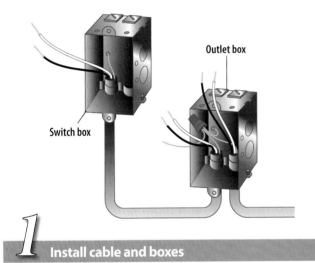

Outlet box

Switch box

1 Install cable and boxes

Shut off the power. Disconnect the receptacle and run two-wire cable to a switch box. Hook up the ground wires.

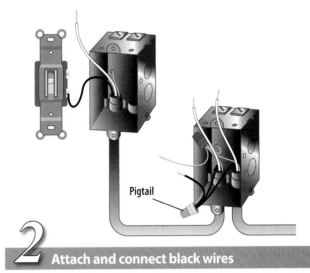

Pigtail

2 Attach and connect black wires

Route power to the switch by tying the two black wires together with a pigtail at the receptacle box. Connect the black wire to the switch.

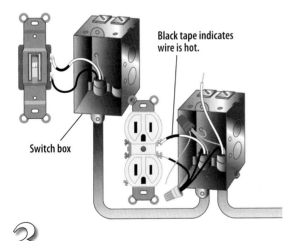

Black tape indicates wire is hot.

Switch box

3 Continue wiring and split outlets

Add black tape to both ends of the white wire that runs between the boxes to show that it's hot. Connect it to the switch and receptacle terminals. Attach the remaining black wire to the receptacle. Snap off the brass tab with needle-nose pliers to split the outlets. Leave the silver-colored metal tab in place.

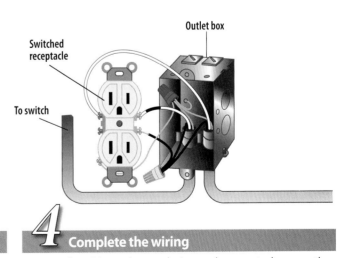

Switched receptacle

Outlet box

To switch

4 Complete the wiring

Connect the white and ground wires to the receptacle, screw the receptacle and switch to their boxes, turn on the power, and test. In this example the upper outlet will be live only when the switch is on. The lower one remains on at all times.

Installing surface-mounted wiring

- **TIME:** About 4 hours for a system like the one shown
- **SKILLS:** Connecting wires, measuring and cutting
- **TOOLS:** Tape measure, hacksaw and miter box, level, basic electrician's tools

I f you do not want to cut into your walls, fish wires, and patch and paint after adding a fixture, consider surface-mounted wiring. Surface-mounted components are available in metal or plastic and are comparatively easy to install. The system's main drawback is that it is fully visible. But for informal settings—a basement or a workroom, for instance—it is a convenient alternative.

Shut off the power before connecting to existing receptacles.

BASEBOARD CHANNEL

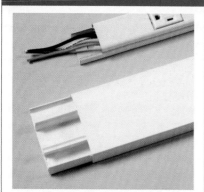

A decorative and functional plastic baseboard channel can be added to an existing baseboard or even substituted for it. This type of channel is designed to simultaneously carry household wiring, coaxial cable, and telephone and computer lines. Extension boxes with receptacles, phone jacks, and coaxial hookups can be added along its length.

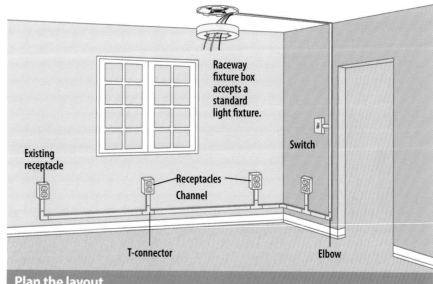

Raceway fixture box accepts a standard light fixture.

Switch

Existing receptacle

Receptacles

Channel

T-connector

Elbow

Plan the layout

Check your local codes; they probably limit surface, or raceway, wiring to dry locations where it will not be susceptible to damage (as it might be, for example, in a garage). Decide where you want the pieces to go and measure carefully for all the runs. Take your calculations to your home center or electrical supplier and have a salesperson help you choose the parts you need.

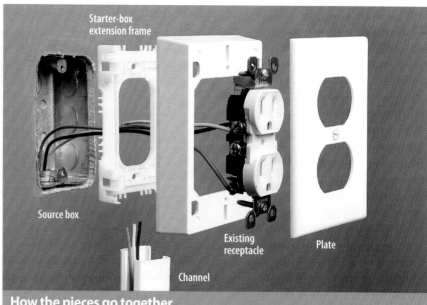

Starter-box extension frame

Source box

Existing receptacle

Channel

Plate

How the pieces go together

A raceway system begins by tapping into an existing circuit at a receptacle. Select a receptacle on a circuit that has enough capacity for additional outlets (see pages 134–135). Install a starter box on the existing outlet so it can match up with the wall-mounted channel. Knockout holes allow you to extend the raceway channel from the starter box in any direction. Additional receptacles—as well as switches and light fixtures—mount directly on the wall or ceiling.

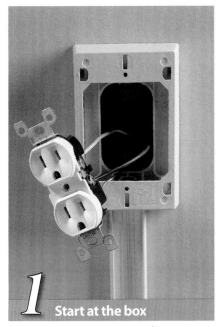

1 Start at the box

Shut off the power. Remove the receptacle and install the starter box. The receptacle will be reinstalled in the starter box later, as shown in step 5. Map out the system from this starting point.

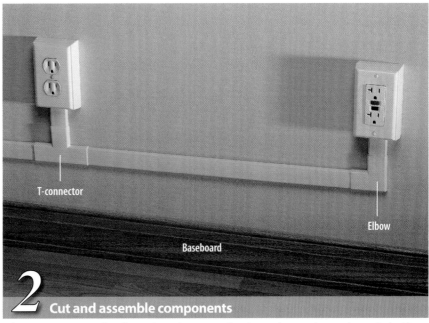

T-connector

Elbow

Baseboard

2 Cut and assemble components

When you measure the channel sections for cutting, take into account the elbows, Ts, and other connectors. Cut the channels with a hacksaw and a miter box. Use extension connectors to tie the ends of the channels together and attach the Ts and the elbows at the corners. Measure carefully from the floor and use a level to make sure the receptacles are the same height.

3 Attach parts securely

Chances are the channels will be bumped by furniture and normal household traffic, so take care to attach them securely. Locate studs and drill screws into them where possible. Use plastic anchors in places you can't reach the studs.

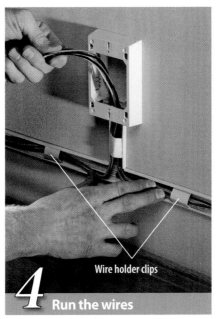

Wire holder clips

4 Run the wires

Run the wiring and hold it in place approximately every foot with specially designed clips. Leave 6 to 8 inches of wire at each outlet for room to strip and make the connections.

5 Make the connections

Attach all fixtures and receptacles. Connect the circuit to the existing receptacle, turn the power back on, and test the new fixtures and receptacles. Install the snap-on covers for the channels, fittings, and boxes.

Installing a fan-rated ceiling box

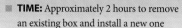

- **TIME:** Approximately 2 hours to remove an existing box and install a new one
- **SKILLS:** Basic carpentry skills, connecting cable
- **TOOLS:** Hammer, pry bar, keyhole or reciprocating saw, screwdriver, drill with screwdriver bit, wrench

A ceiling fan is heavy and vibrates continuously as it runs, so it must be firmly attached to the ceiling. The best approach is to install a fan-rated ceiling box designed to handle the extra load. A fan-rated box is also a good choice for installing any heavy fixture, such as a large chandelier.

The box may be either metal or a durable plastic. It should have deep, threaded screw holes to securely attach the mounting bolts.

CEILING FAN CLEARANCES AND CAPACITY

For safety—and to give the fan adequate space to effectively move air—use the clearances shown below. Select fan blades to suit the square footage of the room.

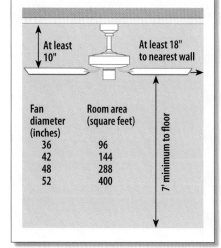

At least 10"
At least 18" to nearest wall
7' minimum to floor

Fan diameter (inches)	Room area (square feet)
36	96
42	144
48	288
52	400

Removing a ceiling box

Shut off the power. If the space above is an unfinished attic, disconnect the box from the attic. If you need to work from below, take care not to damage any wiring. You may need to enlarge the hole to get at the box. (You can install a medallion later to cover up the larger hole.) Use a reciprocating saw or a keyhole saw to cut through mounting nails.

Removing an older pancake box

An older box like this may be held in place with screws driven into lath or a joist and with a nut that attaches it to a center pipe. Once you pry out the box, you may need to cut the pipe as well; be careful not to damage the wires.

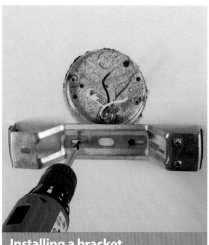

Installing a bracket instead of a box

In some cases you may firmly affix the ceiling fan's mounting plate directly to the ceiling instead of installing a fan-rated box. Drive two or three wood screws (not drywall screws, which are not strong enough) through the mounting plate and deep into a joist. Cover the ceiling box with a medallion.

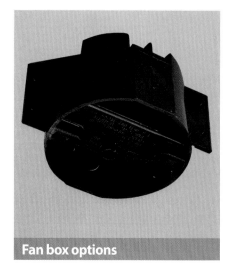

Fan box options

Some fan-rated boxes attach to the side of a joist. Others (as shown on the opposite page) attach between joists. Still others fit directly under the joist.

Installing a braced box

1 Put the box brace in place

A braced box is usually the best choice. The box must be at least 1½ inches away from the side of a joist. If necessary enlarge the hole to accommodate the extra space. Slide the brace (with the box unattached) into the hole.

2 Tighten the brace

Rotate the brace's shaft until it starts to tighten against the joists. Measure to make sure it is centered on the hole and is the correct height so the box will be flush with the ceiling. Firmly tighten the brace with a wrench.

3 Attach the box

Attach the U-bolt assembly onto the shaft; it should be centered on the hole. Clamp the cable to the box. Slide the box over the bolts and tighten the nuts to hold it firmly.

Installing from the attic

If the space above is an unfinished attic, remove the old box from there. Add a new-work fan-rated box. Assemble the box onto the brace, slide the box to the desired location, and fit the brace between joists. Check to make sure the bottom of the box is flush with the ceiling, then drive screws or nails to secure the brace.

Installing a box beneath a joist

If a joist is directly above the hole, running through the hole's center, install the box by driving two or three wood screws (not drywall screws) into the joist.

Installing a ceiling fan

- **TIME:** 3 or 4 hours to install a ceiling fan once the box is installed and wired
- **SKILLS:** Basic wiring skills
- **TOOLS:** Wrench, screwdriver, drill with screwdriver bit, wire stripper, needle-nose pliers

Whether it's moving warm air downward for heat in the winter or circulating cool air in the summer, a ceiling fan can cut energy costs and help keep your home more comfortable all year.

Start with a strong, fan-rated box securely fastened to the ceiling (see pages 112–113). If you want to control the fan and the light separately, you can run three-wire cable from the fan to the switch box or install a remote-control fan.

Lights are an integral part of some fans. Other fans provide the option of having a fan only or installing a light kit that you buy separately.

1 Assemble the fan

Follow the manufacturer's instructions for adding a downrod and installing the canopy. Take care to assemble the pieces in the correct order. Run the fan and light leads through the downrod.

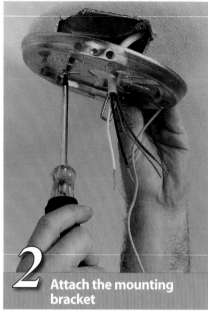

2 Attach the mounting bracket

Shut off the power. Anchor the mounting bracket firmly to the fan-rated box using the screws provided. Some models have rubber washers that sandwich between the bracket and the box to dampen sound and minimize vibration. Tug on the bracket to make sure it is strong.

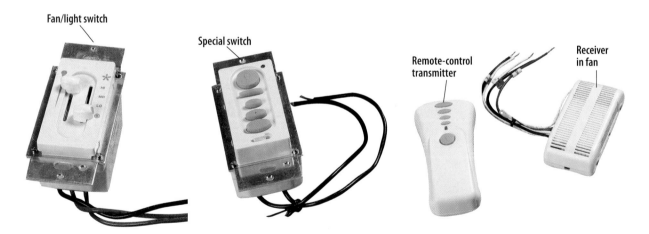

Fan/light switch

Special switch

Remote-control transmitter

Receiver in fan

Switching options

Most ceiling fans have two pull switches, one for the fan and one for the light. If you want to control the light and the fan separately from a wall switch, several options are available at a home center:
- Run three-wire cable from the fixture to the switch box and install a fan/light double switch (shown above left).
- Buy a fan that has a special wall switch that controls the fan and light through a standard two-wire cable (above center).

- Install a wireless remote-control switch (above right). A receiver fits inside the fan's canopy so you can control the fan and the light from anywhere in the room with a wireless transmitter. This is convenient but more expensive. Some fans have built-in wireless remote controls.

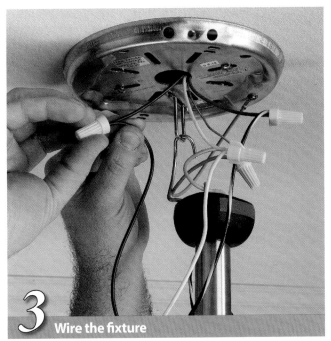

3 Wire the fixture

Most fans have a hook that allows you to hang it temporarily from the bracket while you work. Connect the ground lead (see page 61). If only two wires enter the box, splice the white lead to the white wire and splice both the hot lead for the fan and the hot lead for the light to the black wire. If three wires enter the box, splice black to the fan and red to the light.

4 Add the canopy

It's important that the wires are neatly and securely tucked up and away in the box rather than hanging into the canopy; otherwise they could make noise when the fan runs. Slip the canopy onto the mounting bracket and tighten the screws to hold it firm.

5 Attach the fan blades

Make sure the correct side of the fan blades faces down, then screw a bracket onto each fan blade. Screw the brackets to the fan motor. After they are all installed, go back and tighten them.

6 Wire the light

Remove the cover plate on the bottom of the fan to reveal the wiring for the fan. Find the white wire and the correct colored wire (see your manufacturer's instructions) and connect the leads for the light kit as directed. Tuck the wires back into the housing, push the light onto the housing, and secure with screws.

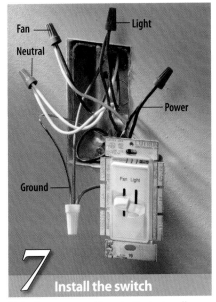

7 Install the switch

If the fan comes with a dedicated wall switch, follow the manufacturer's wiring instructions. If you run three-wire cable from the fan for a double switch, connect the black wire from the fan to the switch's fan lead and the red wire to the switch's light lead. Join the white wires together and splice any ground wires together in the box.

Adding a bathroom vent fan/light

- **TIME:** About a day to install a fan and run ductwork
- **SKILLS:** Basic electrical skills, carpentry skills
- **TOOLS:** Drywall saw or jigsaw, screwdriver, drill, lineman's pliers, wire stripper

A vent fan removes moisture and odor from a bathroom. Most models come with a light as well, and some also include a nightlight or a heat lamp. A unit with a heat lamp may require a separate circuit because it uses much more amperage.

You can put the fan and the light on separate switches, but some codes require the fan to switch on with the light.

Identify venting options

Plan the route of the vent before you start installation. The shorter and straighter the duct run, the better the fan will suck air out of the bathroom and send it outside. A wall or eave vent, such as the one pictured here, is easiest to install. If necessary you can install a vent on the roof. Avoid cutting joists, wall studs, or roof-truss members so you won't weaken your framing.

1 Cut a hole in the ceiling

Shut off the power. If you have an existing light fixture, remove the ceiling box. Use the fan's housing as a template to mark for the hole, next to a joist. Cut the hole (either from above or below) using a drywall saw or jigsaw.

2 Attach the fan body

Disassemble the fan. If the fan requires three-wire cable, run it from the switch box to the fan. If insulation is present cut pieces of lumber to fit between the joists and install them to keep the insulation several inches away from the fan. Hold the fan so its bottom edge is flush with the ceiling and fasten it to the joists with screws or nails.

3 Install a vent cap

Use a long bit to drill a locator hole from inside the attic. From the outside cut a hole for the vent cap using a jigsaw or reciprocating saw. Attach a length of duct to the vent cap, fastening it with screws and professional-quality duct tape. Run a bead of caulk around the hole and slide the vent cap to the wall. Attach it with screws or nails.

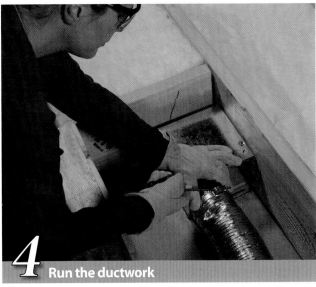

4 Run the ductwork

Run solid or flexible ducting from the vent cap to the fan. If possible use a short, straight piece. If you use flexible ducting, cut it precisely to length rather than allowing it to loop around or bunch up. Fasten the joints with clamps, then wrap with duct tape.

5 Wire the fan

Reassemble the fan. Strip the sheathing and the wire ends and clamp the cable to the fan housing. Connect the wiring according to manufacturer's directions. Connect the grounds and splice the white wires together. For a fan/light that is controlled by separate switches, connect the fan's lead to the black wire and the light's lead to the red wire.

6 Wire the switch

See page 16 for basic ways to wire a switch. If power enters the switch box and separate switches will control the light and the fan, connect the grounds and splice the white wires. Put two pigtails on the feeder wire and connect them to the brass terminals. Attach the red wire to one silver terminal and the black wire to the other silver terminal.

TIMER SWITCH FOR A FAN

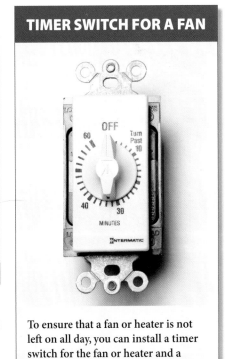

To ensure that a fan or heater is not left on all day, you can install a timer switch for the fan or heater and a standard switch for the light. You will need a double-gang box.

Installing an attic fan

■ **TIME:** A full day, with a helper
■ **SKILLS:** Basic electrical and carpentry skills
■ **TOOLS:** Ladder to get to the roof, roof jacks to provide a safe standing place if the roof is steep, drill, jigsaw or reciprocating saw, utility knife, hammer, screwdriver, lineman's pliers

On a hot summer day, the temperature in an attic can reach 150 degrees F or more. Turbine-type roof ventilators can help, but because they depend on wind to supplement the upward draft of hot air, you're out of luck on a still day when the heat buildup may be most intense.

A thermostat-controlled attic fan, mounted in the roof or a gable-end wall, automatically turns the fan on to vent overheated attics.

HOW BIG A FAN DO YOU NEED?

To determine how powerful a unit to buy, multiply the square footage of your attic by 0.7. Add 15 percent if your roofing is dark-colored—it will absorb more heat from sunlight than a lighter, more reflective roofing color. The resulting number tells you the cubic feet per minute (CFM) that your fan should pull.

1 Drill a locating hole

Position your fan as close to the ridge as you can to minimize the amount of hot air that will build up in the attic area above the fan. Choose a slope of the roof that's not visible from the street. Go into the attic and pick a pair of rafters close to the attic's center. Measure to a point midway between them. Drill up through the roof at this point. Leave the drill bit in place or push a piece of wire up through the hole as a marker.

2 Cut a hole for the fan

The manufacturer will provide a template or exact dimensions for the hole. You may adjust the position of the hole up or down a few inches in order to minimize the number of shingles you need to cut. Cut through the roofing and the sheathing using a reciprocating saw or a heavy-duty jigsaw. You may need to trim back some shingles as well.

COMBINE WHOLE-HOUSE FANS AND ATTIC FANS

Depending on your climate and use pattern, it may make economic sense to combine a thermostat-controlled fan with a whole-house fan. Here's why:

Even after sundown super-heated air continues to put a heavy strain on your home's air-conditioning system. By improving attic ventilation you can cut cooling costs as much as 30 percent.

A whole-house fan will pull a strong, steady draft up through the house—and push air out of the attic—on those days when you choose not to use the air-conditioning. It is not, however, effective to use a whole-house fan while the air-conditioning is operating.

Gable fan

You may choose to install a gable fan rather than a roof-mounted fan, especially if you already have a louvered cutout in the gable. It's easier to install because you don't have to cut a hole in the roof. Position it as high as possible and wire it as you would a roof fan.

3 Install the fan

Pry up under shingles to loosen and remove roofing nails so you can slip the fan's flange all the way in. Slide the fan into position, centered over the hole.

4 Attach and weatherproof it

The upper two-thirds of the fan's flange should be covered with shingles; the lower one-third should rest on top of the shingles. Drive roofing nails as recommended by the manufacturer and coat any exposed nails with roofing cement.

5 Attach the thermostat

Back in the attic screw the thermostat switch to a stud or rafter above the fan and out of the air stream it will create. Remove the box cover plate.

6 Make the wiring connections

Run cable from a junction box to the thermostat. Install cable to an accessible switch that can be used to override the automatic control. Follow the fan manufacturer's instructions for wiring.

7 Test and adjust

Turn on the power and test your installation. An adjusting screw in the thermostat box lets you set the temperature that will activate the fan. The temperature setting will vary depending on your roof and the fan's capacity. Consult the manufacturer's instructions for the right temperature for your attic.

BUILDING A DEFENSE AGAINST HUMIDITY

If your area has high humidity, consider an attic fan with both a humidistat and thermostat. A humidistat senses humidity in the same way a thermostat reads the temperature, giving you another measurement for controlling the comfort level of your home.

On humid days an attic fan can make your home more comfortable by removing some of the moist air. Keeping attic moisture under control also helps prevent your fiberglass insulation from compacting and losing its effectiveness.

Installing a whole-house fan

■ **TIME:** About a day if fishing the cable is straightforward
■ **SKILLS:** Basic electrical and carpentry skills
■ **TOOLS:** Drill, saber saw, drywall saw, screwdriver, lineman's pliers, wire stripper

Before you select a whole-house fan, plan the overall venting of your house. The fan should pull air through open windows and doors on the lower floors and out through vents in the attic, eaves, and gables. Without adequate openings below and above the fan, it will not be able to do its job. Leave at least 2 feet of clearance between the fan and any obstructions. If you stack your attic with boxes, the fan may not have room to breathe, which will make it noisy as well as inefficient. Installation is not as difficult as you may think: The fan sits on top of the joists in the attic, so cutting and reframing aren't necessary.

CHOOSING A FAN

Buy a fan that's rated to pull a minimum cubic feet per minute (CFM) equal to the square footage of your house multiplied by three.

Will you really vent the whole house? If you plan to open the windows of just a few rooms, use only their square footage to figure the needed CFM.

Often a hall is the best spot for a fan. Will it fit yours? Fans designed to vent houses larger than 1,800 square feet (5,400 CFM) generally have louver panels of 38 inches or more—too wide for some hallways.

1 Establish a location

Find a spot for the fan—the top-floor hallway ceiling is the usual place. Measure from a point common to the hall and the attic, choose a location for the fan, and clear away the insulation. Beside the joists drill locator holes for cutting away the drywall or plaster. Cut a hole in the ceiling from below. Don't cut any joists.

2 Install the fan

Remove any insulation that is in the way. You may need to install pieces of blocking to fill the spaces between the joists; or install plastic baffles supplied with the fan. (There should be no open space on the sides.) Build a frame of flat-laid 2×4s on top of the joists. Set the fan on top. Fasten it firmly with screws so it will not vibrate.

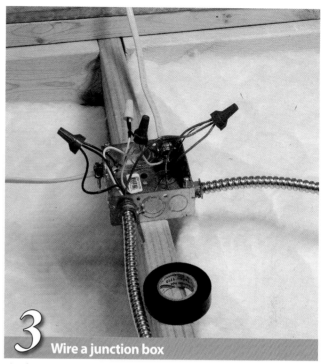

3 Wire a junction box

The fan may have a short length of armored cable. If a junction box is not close enough for the cable to reach, install one. **Shut off the power.** Bring power to the box via two-wire cable; make sure the fan will not overload the circuit (see page 10). Clamp the fan's cable to the box and also run cable to a switch box in the room below. Follow the fan manufacturer's wiring instructions.

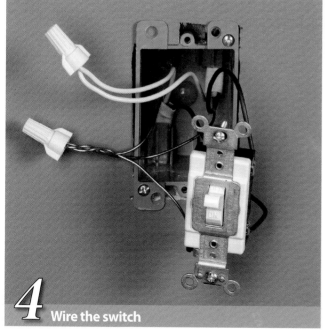

4 Wire the switch

Shut off the power. If no power is available in the attic, you can run power to the switch box first. Consult the manufacturer's fan instructions for wiring diagrams. Some fans have power dampers, two-speed motors, and other features that require specific switches and wiring.

5 Install the cover

From below position the louver panel up against the ceiling so it covers the hole. Attach it to the ceiling by driving screws up into the joists. Test the louvers to make sure they open and close freely.

Installing a range hood

■ **TIME:** Most of a day to run ducting outside, run cable, and install the range hood
■ **SKILLS:** Basic carpentry skills, basic electrical skills
■ **TOOLS:** Hammer, lineman's pliers, drywall saw, drill, jigsaw or reciprocating saw, screwdriver, wire stripper, tin snips

A typical range hood has a light and also a fan that sucks smoke and odors out of the kitchen. The fan and the light are controlled by a switch on the fan, so it is not necessary to install a wall switch.

The bottom of the range hood should be about 24 inches above the range, or 60 inches above the floor. Usually it is attached to the underside of a wall cabinet that is 30 inches above the range.

Duct options

For maximum efficiency run the ducting directly to the outside. Usually that means going straight out the back. In some situations, however, you may need to run ducting up and through the attic.

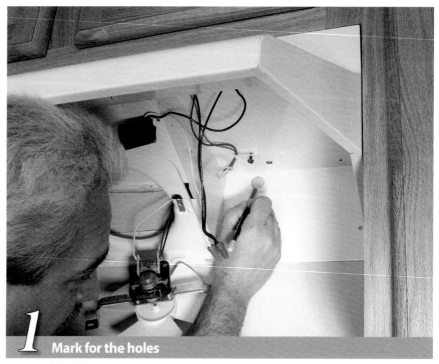

1 Mark for the holes

Disassemble the fan and use a hammer and pliers to remove the knockouts for the vent and the cable. Hold the fan housing in place and trace the locations of the two holes.

2 Cut the holes

Cut the drywall or plaster with a drywall saw or jigsaw. Equip a drill with a long bit, and drill four locator holes through to the outside.

3 Cut the siding

On the outside hold the end cap up against the siding to make sure the locator holes are correct; you may need to enlarge or narrow the hole slightly. Cut the hole using a jigsaw or a reciprocating saw.

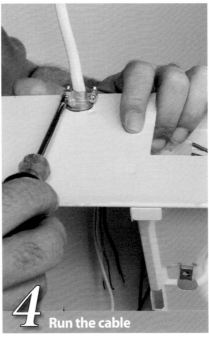

4 Run the cable

Shut off the power. Run two-wire cable from a power source and through the hole in the wall. Strip the sheathing and clamp the cable to the range hood's housing.

5 Install the end cap and duct

Cut the duct so it will reach the fan and attach it to the end cap by driving screws and wrapping with professional-quality duct tape. Run a bead of caulk around the hole and insert the duct through the hole. Press the end cap against the wall and drive screws to secure it.

6 Attach the housing

Install the damper unit onto the housing. Position the housing and slide it so the duct fits over the damper unit. Drive four screws up through the housing and into the cabinet to secure it.

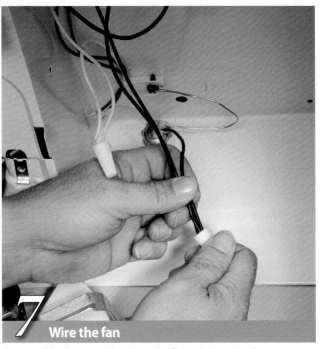

7 Wire the fan

Reassemble the range hood. In the fixture's junction box, connect the ground wires. Splice the white lead to the white wire and the black lead to the black wire. Tuck the wires in and replace the cover plate.

Installing telephone and TV wiring

■ **TIME:** One hour for a typical extension of a television cable or telephone line
■ **SKILLS:** Connecting wires, possibly some carpentry skills
■ **TOOLS:** Drill, screwdriver, pliers, wire stripper, carpentry tools

Telephone and cable (or satellite) TV companies will install extension wiring for you, but they may charge a hefty amount, even for running a simple surface-mounted extension line. Although it is not feasible for a homeowner to make extensive installations, it does make sense for you to run cable for extra telephones or a second TV. Before you add cable TV outlets, check with your cable TV provider to make sure you are allowed to add hardware and additional lines to the installation in your home.

You'll find that running wires for telephones and cable TV is easier than electrical wiring. There is no danger of shock and only one cable to run. Still the same principles of installation and connection apply: Protect wire insulation from damage and secure the connections.

The simplest way to install the cable is to tack or staple it to the wall. Although a common practice this can be unsightly and a mess when you paint walls and molding. For a neater and more permanent installation, take the time to run the cable out of sight as shown on the opposite page.

Telephone and cable jacks

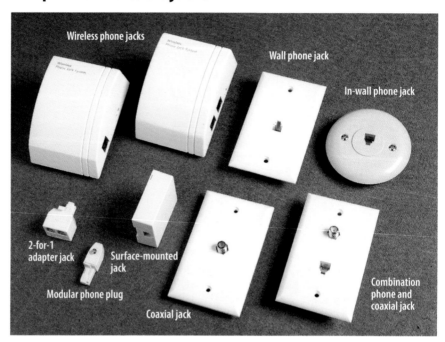

Wireless phone jacks
Wall phone jack
In-wall phone jack
2-for-1 adapter jack
Surface-mounted jack
Modular phone plug
Coaxial jack
Combination phone and coaxial jack

Telephone and television cable

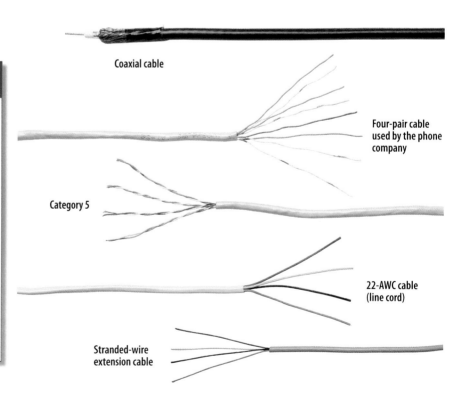

Coaxial cable
Four-pair cable used by the phone company
Category 5
22-AWC cable (line cord)
Stranded-wire extension cable

THE RIGHT CABLE

To avoid a noisy connection and possible damage to your phone system, use cable marked 22-AWC (often marked "line cord") or "Category 5" to add a branch line. This solid-core cable is more expensive than stranded wires or filament wire, but well worth the investment. Stranded-wire extension cable, sold in 25- and 50-foot lengths, should only be used between the jack and the phone, not for adding new extensions.

Purchase shielded coaxial cable for television cables. It has a metal wrapping under the insulation. Nonshielded cable will probably cause interference and distortion.

Installing a wall phone or cable jack

1 Locate the jack

Cut a hole in the wall where you want to locate an in-wall phone or cable jack. Run cable along the wall to a point directly below the box location. Make sure you have plenty of extra cable to reach from the floor to the new jack. Drop a length of beaded chain down through the hole. If you feel it hitting an obstruction, wiggle it to try to get past the problem.

2 Grab the chain at the bottom

Once the chain drops far enough, drill a hole in the wall at the point where you want to feed in the cable. (To hide the cable completely, remove the baseboard molding first.) Insert a bent piece of coat hanger wire and root around until you hook the chain. Pull the chain through the hole and attach to the cable with electrician's tape.

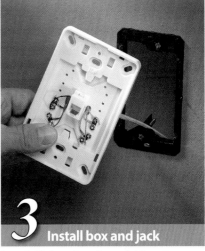

3 Install box and jack

Install the box. For phone cable strip the sheathing and insulation and make connections as marked on the jack. At the phone junction box, connect the wires to the color-coded terminals. Secure the cable to the wall or baseboard. Pull the top of the chain until about 8 inches of cable protrudes through the box hole.

Hide cable under carpeting

If you don't want to go to the trouble of pulling up your baseboard, it is often possible to hide most of the cable under wall-to-wall carpeting. Pry up only 2 feet of carpeting at a time or you may have trouble getting it to reattach to the tack strip. Slip the cable underneath the carpet and push it firmly back in place as you go.

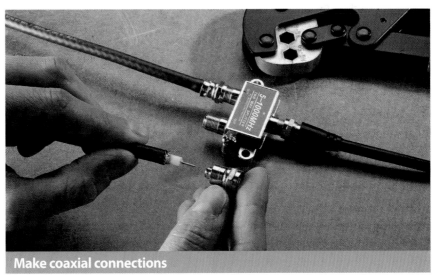

Make coaxial connections

To make any type of coaxial connection, first attach male connectors to each cut cable end: Using strippers or a knife, strip $\frac{1}{2}$ inch of outer sheathing; cut carefully so the underlying wire mesh stays intact. Fold back the wire mesh and strip $\frac{3}{8}$ inch of the plastic insulation. Slip on a crimp-type connector. The wire should run about $\frac{1}{16}$ inch past the connector. Use a special coaxial crimping tool (above) to crimp the connection tight.

Once the male connectors are attached, you can screw them onto a fitting, such as the splitter, above.

Installing home security devices

■ **TIME:** About 1 hour for a doorbell intercom; several hours to install an alert system with 7 or 8 sensing devices
■ **SKILLS:** No special skills required
■ **TOOLS:** Screwdriver, drill

After you've installed solid locks on your doors and outdoor lighting (see pages 130–132), the next step toward a safer home is to add some electric security devices. Home centers often do not carry a wide choice of these products, but a visit to an electronics store or the Internet will reveal an array of possible devices.

The doorbell intercom on this page runs via your existing doorbell wires, and the intruder alert system on the opposite page is wireless, making both of these solutions easy to install.

INTERCOM OPTIONS

If you do not have functioning doorbell wires, consider a wireless intercom system. The intercom at the door communicates with one or more intercoms located anywhere in the house. You can also set up the system so the various indoor intercoms can communicate with each other.

Another system connects to telephone lines so when a person at the door pushes the button, your phones ring. You can pick up any phone and talk to the intercom.

Installing a doorbell intercom

1 Install the doorbell module

Remove the doorbell button and disconnect the wires. Clip the wires so they cannot slip back down the hole. Fasten the mounting bracket. Attach the bell wires to the terminal screws on the back of the doorbell module and mount the module.

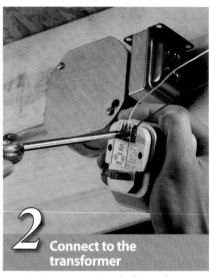

2 Connect to the transformer

Locate the existing doorbell transformer in your home (see pages 40–41). Transfer the wires from its terminals to the new AC adapter that comes with the system. Plug the adapter into the nearest 120-volt receptacle. This links the doorbell module to the circuit that will carry the signal to the intercom monitor.

3 Disconnect the chime or bell

Take off the doorbell or chime cover. Unscrew the terminal screws and remove the wires. Twist the bare ends of the wires together and cover the splice with a small wire nut. Because you will no longer need it, remove the doorbell.

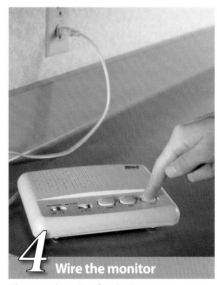

4 Wire the monitor

Choose a location for the intercom monitor and fasten it to the wall with the screws provided. Then hang the unit in place and plug its cord into a receptacle.

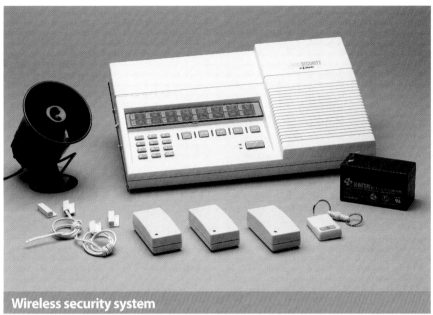

Wireless security system

You can install a wireless security system for far less than it costs to have the pros do it. A typical console has 10 zones of wireless protection. Each zone is controlled by a single sensor, which may be a door/window sensor, a contact sensor, a motion detector, or a glass-break detector. When a sensor is activated, a loud siren sounds. You can set the console for protection while you are at home or away. A keychain remote control allows you to turn the alarm on or off as you enter or leave the house. A rechargeable backup battery provides power when the electricity is off.

Install a door/window sensor

Place the small part of the sensor on the door or window and position the larger portion on the wall so that the two parts are aligned when the door or window is closed. Attach by driving screws.

Glass-break detector

Use this unit where an intruder may enter by breaking the glass—for example, a large first-floor window or a sliding glass door. It attaches to the glass via a suction cup.

Motion detector

This unit triggers the alarm when it senses motion. Install it about 3 feet above the floor near a main or rear entrance or in a hallway.

Adding 240-volt receptacles

■ **TIME:** About 1 hour to install a 240-volt receptacle after the wiring is completed
■ **SKILLS:** Running cable, stripping and connecting wires
■ **TOOLS:** Screwdriver, wire stripper, lineman's pliers

S ome 240-volt equipment—central air-conditioning units and electric water heaters, for example—have no plugs and are wired directly into junction boxes because they do not need to be moved. Ranges, dryers, and other appliances have cords and plugs that require special receptacles.

The wiring requirements for 240-volt circuits are specific. For a 30-amp dryer, use a 30-amp breaker and 10-gauge wire. For a 50-amp range, use a 50-amp breaker and 6-gauge wire. Choose a receptacle designed to provide the correct amperage for your appliance and with holes to match the prongs on the plug.

CAUTION

DANGER: HIGH VOLTAGE!
Wiring for 240-volt receptacles is no different from regular 120-volt lines, except that the danger is much, much greater. Even if you are dry and wearing rubber-soled shoes, a jolt of this current could seriously harm or even kill you. Check and double-check that the power is off before installing a 240-volt receptacle. This is one job where you may want to call in an experienced electrician, just for safety's sake.

240-volt wiring

Shut off the power. Wiring starts at a 240-volt breaker or fuse at the service panel and ends at a specially designed receptacle. A 240-volt circuit should supply only one appliance; no other receptacles can be attached to it. Connect 120-volt wires to a breaker and the neutral wire to the neutral bus bar (see pages 136–137).

Floor-mounted 240-volt receptacle

If no outlet box is available, you can install this unit on the floor. Position it so it won't get bumped when you move the appliance. Remove the cover and connect the neutral wire to the terminal marked "white" and the red and black wires to the other terminals. The neutral wire serves as the ground for this receptacle.

Dryer receptacle

Install a box and run 10/3 cable or four 10-gauge wires through conduit from a 30-amp, 240-volt double breaker in the service panel to the box. Connect the ground wire (see pages 60–61). Strip and connect the other three wires to the terminals.

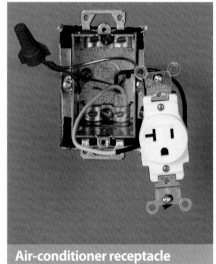

Air-conditioner receptacle

Many large air-conditioners plug into a 20-amp, 240-volt receptacle. Install a box and run 12/2 cable or three 12-gauge wires from a 20-amp, 240-volt double breaker in the service panel to the box. Connect the ground wire (see pages 60–61). Mark the white wire black. Strip the wires and connect them to the terminals.

Adding outdoor receptacles

■ **TIME:** Approximately 3 hours, barring unexpected obstacles

■ **SKILLS:** Basic electrical skills

■ **TOOLS:** Drill with spade bit and perhaps a bit extension; jigsaw or keyhole saw; screwdriver, lineman's pliers, wire stripper. If you have a masonry exterior, a masonry bit, cold chisel, and hammer

The easiest way to bring power to the outside of your house is to install a receptacle directly behind an existing interior receptacle. If you need to place the outdoor receptacle elsewhere, see pages 66–68 for ideas on fishing the cable. Be sure that the interior receptacle box you choose has room for new wires. Check to make sure you will not overload the circuit (see page 10). Codes usually require a GFCI receptacle with a weatherproof cover plate and a spring-loaded door.

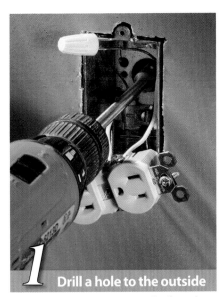

1 Drill a hole to the outside

Shut off the power. Remove the faceplate and the interior outlet. To accurately locate your new receptacle, create a knockout hole in the back of the box and drill a hole through the house to the outside. If the wall is not thick enough to mount boxes back to back, you will have to offset them. Angle the drill off to the side.

2 Cut the exterior opening

Find the hole on the outside of your house and draw an outline of the new box (see page 64). Drill a hole at each corner of the box and cut with a jigsaw. If you have a masonry exterior, drill a series of closely spaced holes with a masonry bit. Knock out the hole with a cold chisel and hammer.

3 Connect the cable

Cut a piece of cable long enough to allow you working room. Connect it to the interior box—you will need a helper to reach through the exterior hole and hold the locknut in position while you tighten the locknut. Attach the cable to the exterior box.

4 Make the electrical connections

With the box pushed into place, strip the sheathing and the ends of the wires and make connections on both ends of the cable (see page 87). Be sure to connect to the "line" terminals on the GFCI receptacle and the load terminals on the existing interior receptacle.

5 Install the box and cover

Attach the box firmly in place. With a masonry wall insert screws into the back of the box and attach them to a framing member or mortar the box in place. Fasten the GFCI receptacle to the box. Finally add the gasket and weatherproof cover plate.

Installing outdoor lighting

I f you have eaves overhanging an exterior door, it makes sense to install a light there, where it will be better protected from weather than a wall-mounted unit would be. You're also likely to find it easy to run cable from an attic junction box to the eaves.

Consider installing a motion-detector floodlight. These are inexpensive, and if you wire it to be controlled with a regular wall switch, you can turn off the motion-sensing feature.

■ **TIME:** Approximately 4 hours, barring unexpected obstacles
■ **SKILLS:** Basic electrical skills, measuring and cutting eaves
■ **TOOLS:** Drill, saber saw or keyhole saw, fish tape, screwdriver, lineman's pliers, wire stripper

CAREFULLY ADJUST MOTION SENSOR

Adjusting a motion-sensor light is best done at night. Aim the light so it helps you but doesn't bother neighbors or passersby. Then set the light-on time; many lights offer 2, 5, or 10 minutes.

Point the motion sensor toward the protected area and set the range control to the middle position. Walk toward the light to see when it turns on. At the same time make sure it does not come on when you don't want it to—for instance, when you walk by on the sidewalk. Aim the motion sensor or adjust the range control to get it right.

1 **Cut a hole in the eaves**

Shut off the power. Draw an outline of the new box. (A retrofit box with wings for attaching to the eaves will probably work best.) Drill starter holes, then cut the hole with a saber saw or a keyhole saw.

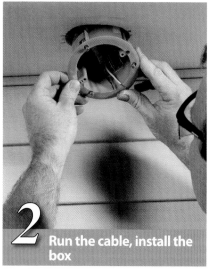

2 **Run the cable, install the box**

Fish cable and make connections to an interior switch (see page 101). Connect the cable to the new box and firmly attach the box to the eaves.

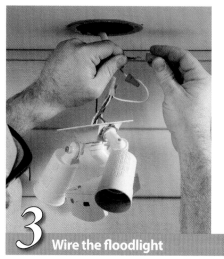

3 **Wire the floodlight**

Connect the wires to the floodlight using wire connectors and screw the light firmly to the box. If your unit has a motion

detector, wait until nighttime and adjust it so it turns on as people approach the door.

Adding low-voltage outdoor lighting

■ **TIME:** Several hours to install a transformer and 10 to 15 lights
■ **SKILLS:** No special skills required
■ **TOOLS:** Shovel, wire stripper, screwdriver, drill with screwdriver bit

These lights are inexpensive and very easy to install. They are not as bright as standard-voltage lights, but they provide enough illumination to light a path or showcase landscaping.

Plan the route of your lights and decide how many you need. Then purchase a kit that contains the lights, the cable, and a transformer. You will need to plug the transformer into a GFCI-protected receptacle. If you need a new outdoor receptacle, see page 129.

LIGHT OPTIONS

You will find a wide selection of low-voltage lights for outdoor use at your local home center. Path lights direct illumination downward. Well lights barely protrude out of the ground, directing light upward.

1 Place the lights

Determine your layout and arrange the lights where they will go. To insert a light into the ground, first try poking it in. If the ground is hard, slice it with a shovel and poke the light into the slice.

2 Run the cable

Route the cable from the transformer's location to the lights.

Adding low-voltage outdoor lighting *(continued)*

3 Connect the lights

Electrical connections are quick and require no tools. Position the two parts of a light's connector over the cable, then snap them together on the cable.

4 Hide the cable

Because it carries only 12 volts, the wiring is not dangerous. Dig a shallow trench, lay the cable in the trench, and cover it with soil, sod, or mulch.

Solar light

The easiest way to install an outdoor light fixture is to poke a solar light into the ground. It will absorb and store electricity during the day and shine at night.

5 Connect to the transformer

Strip the wire ends and connect them to the transformer's terminals.

6 Install the transformer

Fasten the transformer to the house in a location where it is unlikely to be bumped. Plug into a GFCI receptacle with an in-use watertight cover.

7 Program the transformer

The transformer can be set to turn lights on when it gets dark, or you may choose to program a timer.

Planning paths for new circuits

Electric cable often does not run in a straight line. Instead it zigzags from one outlet to another in a circuit. Sharp turns and long trips do not bother electricity. You can snake cable up and down walls, along or across joists, and around obstructions without impeding the flow of electrons.

In this home two general-purpose 120-volt circuits enter through the bottom plate of the stud wall and travel around perimeter walls to receptacle outlets. Two others go up into the ceiling for lighting, and a 240-volt circuit follows along a floor joist to serve an electric stove receptacle.

Saving money by planning
Even though electricity isn't affected by bends and detours, cable is priced by the foot, and extra feet can add up fast—in extra labor as well as materials. So to be economical keep your runs as short and direct as possible.

In new work that's not too difficult. In this illustration of a well-planned new home (right), most of the cables travel directly to their destinations. The plan saved money by installing the dryer outlet near the service panel, minimizing the amount of heavier, more costly cable needed for its 240-volt circuit.

The plan also saved the electrician time because there was no need for many bends in the conduit to carry the wire through exposed locations. The cable for the 240-volt receptacle for the electric stove, for example, takes as direct a path as possible along the basement sill plate.

Drawing up your plan
In planning an electrical layout, especially if you'll be running more than one circuit, draw a floor plan of your home to scale, then mark the routes the cable will travel. See page 11 for an example of circuits planned for the kitchen and family room, which are two of the more complex areas of a home.

To estimate how much cable you'll need, measure the distances involved and add 10 percent for bends, unexpected detours, and waste. Be sure to add in another 6 to 8 inches to make connections each time cable enters or leaves a junction or outlet box.

Working in finished spaces
If you plan to fish through finished walls and ceilings, be prepared to use more cable than you would if the framing were exposed.

You'll also have to do some detective work. Because cutting holes in walls and patching afterward takes so much time and effort, saving cable is a low priority when wiring in finished space. Search out the path that involves the least damage to your walls and offers the greatest ease in running the cable.

Your first task is to determine what's in the space where you want to run the cable. If it's an exterior wall, for instance, there will probably be insulation, which makes fishing more difficult.

In addition many older homes have fire blocking that spans the studs about halfway up the wall. If faced with these barriers, you will have to notch the wall surface at those points. See pages 66–67 for tips on running cable in finished spaces.

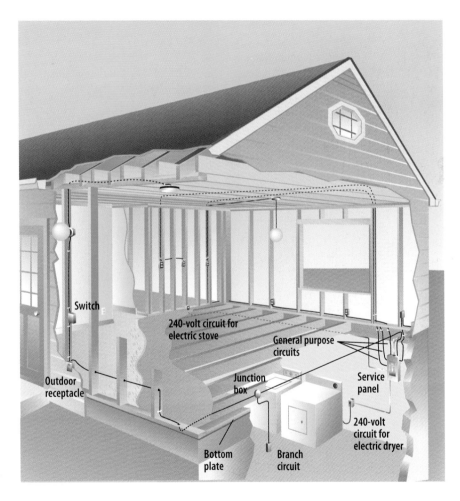

Switch

240-volt circuit for electric stove

General purpose circuits

Outdoor receptacle

Junction box

Service panel

240-volt circuit for electric dryer

Bottom plate

Branch circuit

Planning major circuits

Adding a new circuit to your home's service panel is an advanced project and you may want to call in a professional—especially if your service panel is already crowded. Begin by seeing if you can add to an existing circuit. If not then make sure the service can be expanded. Look for an amperage rating on the main fuse, main circuit breaker, or disconnect switch. Older 60-amp service can't be easily upgraded; call an electrician. Newer 100-amp service may have enough reserve to handle a new circuit or two, and 150- or 200-amp service usually has plenty of capacity.

CIRCUIT CAPACITY

Circuit rating	Maximum capacity	Safe capacity
15 amps	1,800 watts	1,440 watts
20 amps	2,400 watts	1,920 watts
25 amps	3,000 watts	2,400 watts
30 amps	3,600 watts	2,880 watts

1 Add to a circuit

Different circuits have different capacities. If your need for extra capacity is modest, such as a few extra receptacles for a bedroom, see if you can add to a general-purpose or small-appliance circuit. (Never add on to a heavy-duty, single-use circuit.) Figure the entire circuit load by totaling the demand of the appliances and fixtures (see page 10). Then check the chart at left to see if the demand is within a safe capacity. The safe capacity of a circuit, as prescribed by the National Electric Code, is 20 percent less than maximum capacity.

2 Estimate capacity needed

If you can't add to an existing circuit, check the chart at right for the capacity your new circuit likely needs. Rooms such as living rooms and bedrooms with about 10 light or receptacle outlets require only 15-amp capacity. Ideally you should have one general-purpose circuit for every 500 square feet of living space. Some local codes require that lighting and receptacles be on separate general-purpose circuits.

The kitchen is appliance-intensive and needs at least two 20-amp circuits. A bathroom needs one 20-amp circuit protected by a ground fault circuit interrupter. A bathroom receptacle circuit can serve only one bathroom. The garage may require a 20-amp circuit, depending on what equipment will be used there. Laundry room and workshop circuits should have 20-amp capacity.

CIRCUIT NEED SELECTOR

Location	Circuits
Living and dining rooms, bedrooms, hallways, finished basements	A 15-amp general-purpose circuit for each 500 square feet. Separate circuits for lights and receptacles may be required by code. For a room air-conditioner, install a small-appliance circuit.
Kitchen	At least two 20-amp small-appliance circuits and a 15-amp lighting circuit. An electric range needs a 240-volt circuit. A microwave oven may need its own circuit.
Bathroom	A separate 20-amp receptacle circuit for each bathroom; lights must be on a different circuit.
Garage	A 15- or 20-amp general-purpose circuit (depending on tools and machinery, if any) with GFCI protection.
Laundry	A 20-amp small-appliance circuit for the washer and a gas dryer. An electric dryer needs a 240-volt circuit.
Workshop	A 20-amp GFCI circuit; for larger shops run two 20-amp circuits or a separate circuit for lighting.
Outdoors	One 20-amp GFCI circuit.

3 Check the total service capacity

Now that you know what additional circuit capacity you'll need, can your service capacity handle it? If you add up the amperage ratings for all the circuit breakers or fuses, plus the circuits you want to add, you may discover that the total equals or even exceeds the amperage rating of your service panel. Does that mean you can't add new circuits?

Not likely. Few, if any, of the circuits ever work at full amperage capacity. And some of your electrical fixtures and appliances never run at the same time—a furnace blower and an air-conditioner, for example. That's why codes allow you to derate your service capacity. Derating is a standardized reduction used when computing service capacity. The chart shows a derating calculation for a 2,000-square-foot house with 100-amp service, five small-appliance circuits, and two heavy-duty circuits.

In assigning wattage values don't count each general-purpose circuit. Instead use 3 watts per square foot of house area.

DERATING SERVICE CAPACITY

Formula		Derate	
Add		The first 10,000 watts at 100 percent	10,000 W
General-purpose circuits (square footage × 3 watts)	6,000 W	The remaining 13,500 watts at 40 percent	+ 5,400 W
Small-appliance circuits (number × 1,500 watts)	+7,500 W	Derated total	15,400 W
Heavy-duty circuits (total of appliance nameplate ratings in watts)	+10,000 W	**Divide**	
Total	23,500 W	The total derated wattage by voltage	÷240 V
		Derated amperage	64.2 A

Small-appliance circuits rate at 1,500 watts each. Use the full wattage rating for heavy-duty circuits. If two items never run simultaneously, ignore the one that draws less. Rate only the first 10,000 watts of the total at full value, then calculate 40 percent of the remainder. Divide the total by 240 volts. The answer, 64.2 amps, shows that the system could accommodate more circuits.

Double-pole breaker

Tandem breaker

Single-pole breaker

Half-size breaker

4 Check for room in the box

Once you've decided the type and capacity of your new circuit, see if you have room for it in your service panel. If your panel has circuit breakers, you might find a blank space or two. (Unbroken knockouts on the panel indicate space for a breaker underneath.) If there isn't room you may be able to double up two circuits by replacing an existing breaker with a tandem breaker. In a fuse box you might find an unused terminal and socket that could work. More likely you'll have to add a secondary fuse box called a subpanel; consult with a professional.

Adding major circuits

- **TIME:** 3 hours after running the cable to the service panel
- **SKILLS:** Understanding of electrical principles, general electrical skills
- **TOOLS:** Voltmeter, basic electrician's tools

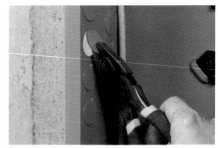

1 Install a new circuit

Shut off the power to the box. Before working on the box, work backward from the new electrical installation. Mount boxes, connect them with cable, and run wiring back to the service panel (see pages 66–68) in what the pros call a "home run." Allow yourself plenty of cable for running wires around the perimeter of the service panel when you install the new breaker.

Your home may have a main disconnect switch, which shuts off power to the service panel. It may be outdoors near the meter. If you have a main disconnect switch, shut it off; now there will be no power in the panel.

If you have no main disconnect, shut off the main breaker. Use a voltage detector to confirm that power is absent in the wires leading to the individual breakers. Work carefully, however, because power is present in the wires that lead to the main breaker.

2 Run cable into the service panel

Remove a knockout plug at a convenient location. Install a cable clamp into the knockout hole. Hold the cable up to the panel to estimate how much wire you will need to run around the perimeter and to the new breaker location and strip more sheathing than you need. Thread the exposed wires through the cable clamp and tighten the clamp.

CAUTION

Remember that the main breaker or main fuse in a service panel does not de-energize the main power cables coming into the box. If you cannot shut off power to the service panel, work carefully or call the power company to disconnect your service temporarily.

OUTDOOR SHUTOFF SWITCHES

An indoor service panel more than 5 feet from the meter requires an outdoor shutoff switch. If you have an outdoor shutoff switch, it's a good idea to keep it secured with a lock. Otherwise anyone passing through your backyard can easily turn off the power to your entire house.

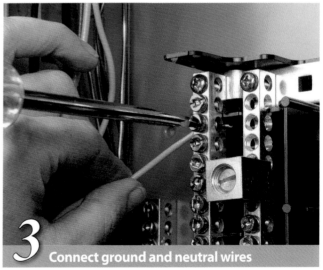

3 Connect ground and neutral wires

Some panels have one bus bar for the neutrals and a separate bar for the grounds; on other panels you connect both neutrals and grounds to the same bar. Route the ground wire to an open terminal, cut it to fit, poke it into the terminal, and tighten the setscrew. Do the same for the neutral wire but strip the wire end before inserting.

4 Hook the hot wire

Route the hot wire to the location of the new breaker and cut it to fit, taking care that the wire will run neatly and stay at the perimeter of the panel as much as possible. Strip ½ inch of insulation, poke the wire into the breaker, and tighten the setscrew.

5 Insert the breaker

Examine nearby breakers to be sure you know how they attach. Push one side of the breaker fully onto one side of the hot bus bar, then push the other side. The breaker should be aligned with its neighbors.

6 Arrange the wires and test

Double-check that none of the wires crosses a hot bar. As far as possible arrange the wires neatly in the panel. Restore power and test all the electrical outlets that are connected to the new circuit. Label the breaker (see page 12).

ADDING A 240-VOLT CIRCUIT

To install a new 240-volt circuit, consult with a professional electrician and check local codes for the correct type of cable and the correct breaker for your situation. Work especially carefully because 240 volts is enough to kill an adult.

Most 240-volt circuits have a white neutral wire and are sometimes called 120/240-volt circuits. The two hot wires—usually red and black—connect to a two-pole breaker and the white wire to the neutral bus bar (right). GFCI breakers install somewhat differently (see page 87).You will need a double-wide space in the panel to accommodate the breaker.

Shut off power and run the cable in a home run from the outlet box to the panel. Clamp the cable securely. Connect the ground and neutral wire to the neutral bus bar. Connect the two hot wires to the breaker—it doesn't matter which wire goes to which pole. Snap the breaker into place, restore power, and test.

Some 240-volt appliances, such as water heaters, do not require a third neutral wire. For this type connect two hot wires to the two-pole breaker and attach the ground wire to the neutral bus bar.

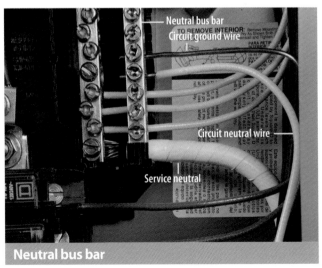

Neutral bus bar

Inside most service panels the white and ground wires for all circuits connect to the neutral bus bar. (No ground wire is used if you are using metal conduit or BX.) The bus bar grounds to the earth through a grounding electrode and connects to the neutral conductor from the service entry.

Glossary

For more information refer to the index on pages 141–143.

Amp (A). A measurement of the amount of electrical current in a circuit at any moment. See also Volt and Watt.

Armored cable. Two or more insulated wires enclosed in a flexible protective metal sheathing.

Ballast. Transformer that steps up the voltage in a fluorescent lamp.

Bell wire. A thin insulated wire used for doorbells. Typically 18-gauge.

Bimetal. Two metals that expand and contract at different rates to open or close a circuit automatically. They are commonly used in circuit breakers and thermostats.

Box. A metal or plastic enclosure within which electrical connections are made and on which devices are mounted. Boxes are made in standard shapes and sizes.

Bus bar. A main power terminal to which circuits are attached in a fuse or breaker box. One bus bar serves the circuit's hot side, the other the neutral side.

BX. An older type of armored cable that contains no ground wire. In a typical installation the metal sheathing itself acts as the ground.

Cable. Two or more insulated conductors wrapped in a flexible metal or plastic outer sheathing.

Circuit. The path of electrical flow from a power source through a load, such as a lamp, and back to ground.

Circuit breaker. A switch that automatically interrupts electrical flow in a circuit in case of an overload or short circuit. Replaces the fuse in modern residential wiring.

Codes. Local regulations and rules governing safe wiring practices. See National Electrical Code.

Common. A terminal on a three-way switch, usually with a dark-colored screw and marked COM.

Conductor. A wire or anything else that carries electricity.

Conduit. Rigid or flexible metal or plastic tubing to contain wires and protect them from damage.

Contact. The point where two electrical conductors touch. The part of a switch which makes or breaks the circuit.

Continuity tester. A device that tells whether a circuit is complete and capable of carrying electricity.

Current. The flow of electricity through a circuit.

Delayed-start tube. A type of fluorescent tube that takes a few seconds to warm up.

Derating. A method for reducing the total service capacity requirement for a residence to account for the fact that circuits are not all in use at their full capacity at the same time.

Device. A switch or receptacle.

Dimmer. A switch that lets you vary the intensity of a light.

Duplex receptacle. A device that includes two plug outlets. Most receptacles in homes are duplexes.

Electrical metallic tubing (EMT). Thin-walled, rigid conduit suitable for indoor use.

Electrons. Invisible particles of charged matter moving at the speed of light through a conductor.

End-wired. A wiring configuration, also called end-line wiring or switch-loop wiring, in which power runs first to the fixture box, and a loop of wire runs to the switch box. See through-switch wiring.

Fishing. Pulling cables through finished walls and ceilings.

Fish tape. A strip of spring steel used for fishing cables and pulling wires through conduit.

Fixture. Any light or other electrical device permanently attached to a home's wiring.

Flexible metal conduit. Tubing that can be bent easily by hand. See Greenfield.

Fluorescent tube. A light source that uses an ionization process to produce ultraviolet radiation. This becomes visible light when it hits the coated inner surface of the tube.

Four-way switch. A type of switch used to control a light from three or more locations.

Fuse. A safety device designed to stop electrical flow if a circuit shorts or is overloaded. Like a circuit breaker, a fuse protects against fire from overheated wiring.

Ganging. Assembling two or more electrical components into a single unit. Boxes, switches, and receptacles often are ganged.

General-purpose circuit. Serves several light and/or receptacle outlets. See Heavy-duty circuit and Small-appliance circuit.

Greenfield. Flexible metal conduit through which wires are pulled.

Ground. Refers to the fact that electricity always seeks the shortest possible path to the earth. Neutral wires carry electricity to ground in all circuits. An additional grounding wire, or the sheathing of metal-clad cable or conduit, protects against shock from a malfunctioning device.

Ground fault circuit interrupter (GFCI). A safety device that senses any shock hazard and shuts down a circuit or receptacle.

Heavy-duty circuit. Serves just one 120- to 240-volt appliance. See General-purpose circuit and Small-appliance circuit.

Hot wire. The conductor that carries current to a receptacle or other outlet. See Ground and Neutral wire.

Incandescent bulb. Light source with a metal filament that glows at white heat.

Insulation. A nonconductive covering that protects wires and other electricity carriers.

Junction box. An enclosure used for splitting circuits into different branches. In a junction box wires connect only to each other, never to a switch, receptacle, or fixture.

Kilowatt (kw). One thousand watts. A kilowatt hour is the standard measure of electrical consumption.

Knockouts. Tabs that can be removed to make openings in a box for cable and conduit connectors.

LB connector or fitting. Elbow for conduit with access for pulling wires.

Leads. Short wires.

MC cable. Armored cable that contains a ground wire, usually green-insulated.

National Electrical Code (NEC). A set of rules governing safe wiring methods drafted by the National Fire Protection Association. Local codes sometimes differ from and take precedence over the NEC.

Neon tester. A device with two leads and a small bulb that determines whether a circuit is carrying current.

Neutral wire. A conductor that carries current from an outlet back to ground. It is clad in white insulation. See Ground and Hot wire.

Nonmetallic sheathed cable. Two or more insulated conductors clad in a plastic covering.

Outlet. Any potential point of use in a circuit, including receptacles, switches, and light fixtures.

Overload. The condition when a circuit carries more amperage than it was designed to handle. Overloading causes wires to heat up and blows fuses or trips circuit breakers.

Polarized plugs. Plugs designed so the hot and neutral sides of a circuit can't be accidentally reversed. One prong of the plug is wider or a different shape than the other.

Raceway wiring. Surface-mounted channels for extending circuits.

Rapid-start tubes. Fluorescent tubes that light up almost instantly.

Receptacle. An outlet that supplies power for lamps and other plug-in devices.

Rigid conduit. Metal tubing to contain wires. It can be bent only with a special tool.

Romex. A trade name for nonmetallic-sheathed cable.

Service entrance. The point where power enters a home.

Service panel. The main fuse or breaker box in a home.

Short circuit. A condition that occurs when hot and neutral wires contact each other. Fuses and breakers protect against fire, which can result from a short.

Small-appliance circuit. Usually has only two or three 20-amp receptacle outlets.

Solderless connectors. Screw-on or crimp-type devices to join two wires.

Stripping. Removing insulation from wire or sheathing from cable.

Stud. An electrical connector. (Also a term referring to a framing member.)

Subpanel. A smaller, subsidiary fuse or breaker box.

System ground. A wire connecting a service panel to the earth. It may be attached to a main water pipe or to a rod driven into the ground.

Three-way switch. Operates a light from two locations.

Glossary *(continued)*

Time-delay fuse. A fuse that does not break the circuit during a momentary overload. If the overload continues the fuse blows.

Through-wired. A wiring configuration in which power travels first-through the switch box and then on to the fixture. See End-wired.

Transformer. A device that reduces or increases voltage. In home wiring, transformers step down current for use with low-voltage equipment such as thermostats and doorbell systems.

Travelers. The conductors that run between three-way switches.

Underwriters knot. A knot used to secure wires in a lamp socket.

Underwriters Laboratories (UL). Independent testing agency that examines electrical components for safety hazards.

Volt (V). A measure of electrical pressure. Volts × amps = watts.

Voltmeter. A device that measures voltage in a circuit.

Wall box. A rectangular enclosure for receptacles and switches. See Junction box.

Watt (W). A measure of the power an electrical device consumes; volts × amps. See Amp, Kilowatt, and Volt.

METRIC CONVERSIONS

U.S. Units to Metric Equivalents			Metric Units to U.S. Equivalents		
To convert from	**Multiply by**	**To get**	**To convert from**	**Multiply by**	**To get**
Inches	25.4	Millimeters	Millimeters	0.0394	Inches
Inches	2.54	Centimeters	Centimeters	0.3937	Inches
Feet	30.48	Centimeters	Centimeters	0.0328	Feet
Feet	0.3048	Meters	Meters	3.2808	Feet
Yards	0.9144	Meters	Meters	1.0936	Yards
Miles	1.6093	Kilometers	Kilometers	0.6214	Miles
Square inches	6.4516	Square centimeters	Square centimeters	0.1550	Square inches
Square feet	0.0929	Square meters	Square meters	10.764	Square feet
Square yards	0.8361	Square meters	Square meters	1.1960	Sqaure yards
Acres	0.4047	Hectares	Hectares	2.4711	Acres
Square miles	2.5899	Square kilometers	Square kilometers	0.3861	Square miles
Cubic inches	16.387	Cubic centimeters	Cubic centimeters	0.0610	Cubic inches
Cubic feet	0.0283	Cubic meters	Cubic meters	35.315	Cubic feet
Cubic feet	28.316	Liters	Liters	0.0353	Cubic feet
Cubic yards	0.7646	Cubic meters	Cubic meters	1.308	Cubic yards
Cubic yards	764.55	Liters	Liters	0.0013	Cubic yards

To convert from degrees Fahrenheit (F) to degrees Celsius (C), first subtract 32, then multiply by 5/9

To convert from degrees Celsius to degrees Fahrenheit, multiply by 9/5, then add 32.

Index